Introduction To Computer Networks
2nd Edition

by

Archana Verma

Introduction To Computer Networks 2nd Edition
by Archana Verma

ISBN: 978-93-62761-25-5

Published by

DOUBLE 9 BOOKS

2/13-B, Ansari Road
Daryaganj, New Delhi – 110002
info@double9books.com
www.double9books.com
Tel. 011-40042856

ABOUT THE AUTHOR

Archana Verma is a highly qualified professional working as an Assistant Professor in the Department of Computer Applications in Noida Institute of Engineering and Technology, Greater Noida, an Autonomous Institute. She has taught a variety of subjects to B.Tech, M.Tech and MCA students for last 22 years. She worked as a software developer in Tata Consultancy Services, Delhi for 6 years prior to that. She obtained Master of Information Science Degree in June 1995 from University of New South Wales, Canberra, Australia. MCA from Maharishi Dayanand University, Rohtak in June 2004 and M.Tech (Computer Science Engineering) from Amity University, Noida in June 2013. She bagged Merit Scholarship award twice while pursuing her MTech. She received Best Teacher Award in the department of Information Technology in 2009. She has written five books, "Unix and Shell Programming", "Bioinformatics", "Database Management Systems", "Operating Systems" and "Introduction to Computer Networks".She has also written a couple of Research Papers and a Book chapter. She is a dedicated teacher and loves her profession. She likes to share her knowledge with students through writing books.

CONTENTS

CHAPTER 3
THE TRANSPORT LAYER

CHAPTER 4
THE NETWORK LAYER

CHAPTER 5
THE DATA LINK LAYER

DEDICATED

To
My Father
Sh. Vidya Sagar Verma

My Sister
Dr. Vandana Verma Marwah

My Brother
Mr. Shashank Verma

My Daughter
Ritambhara

CHAPTER 1
INTRODUCTION TO COMPUTER NETWORKS

1.1 Introduction to Computer Networks

A network is a collection of computers connected to each other. The computers may consist of PCs, servers, Unix workstations, web pages, TVs, mobile phones, environment sensing devices, electrical home appliances. These devices in computer terminology are known as hosts or end devices.

The devices may be connected through a transmission medium. Transmission medium means co-axial cables, copper wire, fibre optics, wireless medium such as Infra Red rays, micro waves and radio waves.

In between the network, there are devices which forward the packets to other interfaces and they are known as routers.

> ISPs (Internet Service Providers) are nodes which are made up of telephone or cable companies. Their main role is to provide internet access to hosts. The ISP is made up of routers, transmission media and the network. Some examples are dial-up-modem, broadband connections and high speed LAN.

To actually work in a network, we require a set of rules that each host follows, and this is known as Protocol. The protocol defines how to interpret the bits sent over the network.

The two most common protocols are TCP and IP. TCP stands for Transmission Control Protocol and IP stands for Internet Protocol. The WWW is known as the Internet, but if an organization wants its own private network, then they can set up an Intranet. An Intranet follows the same protocol as an internet, but the communication is only amongst the routers, hosts, links and transmission media which make up the intranet.

1.2 Protocol

The definition of a protocol is as follows:

A protocol defines the format and the order of messages exchanged between two or more communicating entities, as well as action taken on the transmission and/or receipt of a message or other event.

For example, when bits are transmitted through the physical medium, then both the sender and the receiver agree on how and what bits are sent.

An example in support of this is that suppose we say that a packet is coming of 200 bytes and it has first 20 bytes as its header and the rest as data. So both the sender and the receiver know that the first 20 bytes is header and we can expect the data from the 21st byte to the last byte.

The rate at which the packets are transmitted may be more than what can be absorbed. So this situation is known as congestion and certain protocols are used to take care of this.

The router is a device which forwards packets from source to destination. So it has a protocol based on which it decides how to forward the packets.

1.3 End Systems, Clients and Servers

End Systems are also known as hosts, because they host many application programs. The application programs are as follows:

Web browser, web server , e-mail server etc.

The hosts are also known as clients or servers. A client is a program that sends a request to the server. The server is a program which processes the client request and sends back the answer to the requesting client.

1.4 Characteristics

To communicate, the networks need to have the following characteristics:

1) Delivery: The data must be delivered to the correct destination.

2) Accuracy: The data must be delivered accurately

3) Timeliness: the data must be delivered in a timely manner.

4) Fault Tolerance: Even if there is a breakdown in network, it should keep working with other nodes taking the responsibility to deliver.

5) Scalability: If more nodes want to join the network, then the network should grow and perform equally well

6) Quality of Service: The quality of service should not be degraded, packet loss delays should be handled appropriately.

7) Security: The network should be secure and be able to provide confidentiality, integrity and authentication and availability.

1.5 Components of Data Communication

a) NIC – Network Interface Card

This is a network device which is used to connect computers together on the network. This device contains a MAC address which is encoded on it at the time of manufacture. This MAC address is used to identify a computer uniquely and is stored in the programmable ROM(Read Only Memory). NIC is of two types:

1) Wired NIC

2) Wireless NIC

In wired mode, NIC is present on the motherboard, cables and connectors are used to transfer data. In wireless mode, NIC is in the antenna and obtains connection over wireless medium such as WiFi of the laptop.

b) Repeater

A repeater is a device that boosts the signal which is passed to it. In other words it regenerates the signal. The need to do regeneration is obvious, suppose there is a building or a hill between two stations that need to transmit data. If the data to the other station loses its strength, then we would require a repeater to be installed on the hill so that the signal to the other station is amplified. Repeater operates at physical layer of the OSI model.

c) Hub

A Hub is a node that broadcasts the data to every other computer on the local area network (LAN). It does not provide any routing capability and is only used for forwarding without thinking. Hub operates at physical layer of OSI model. A Hub is also known as a multiport repeater. It connects many nodes to many nodes. A hub operates at physical layer of OSI model.

d) Bridge

They store and forward Ethernet frames. They deal with MAC addresses rather than IP addresses. Here the header of the frame is examined and then forwarded to the proper interface based on destination MAC address. The bridge boosts the signal strength just like a repeater. The bridge has a learning table which keeps account of which machine can be reached through which interface. It is a plug and play device and the hosts are unaware of the presence of the bridges. Bridge operate at data link layer of OSI model.

e) Switch

Switch is also known as multiport bridge. They send, receive or forward the data packets over the network. They have the capability of performing error checking before forwarding. They transmit only the packets which are error free. A switch has multiple ports and has multiple interfaces. This can support unicast, multicast or broadcast communication. They use MAC addresses to transfer data. Switch operates at Data Link Layer of OSI model.

f) Router

Routers have the capacity to transfer packets from LAN to WAN. They are not restricted only to local area network. Routers are used to transfer packets over the network using IP addresses. The routers use a routing table for transferring. The table consists of a set of rules to tell which interface should the packet go to. They operate at network layer of OSI Model.

Suppose we have the following routing table:

IP Address	Subnet Mask	Interface
190.1.2.0	255.255.255.0	S1
190.1.2.64	255.255.255.0	S2
190.1.2.128	255.255.255.0	S3
190.1.2.192	255.255.255.0	S4

We will study the subnet mask in detail later on, for the time being 255 indicates that the corresponding byte in IP address is for the network id and a 0 indicates that the corresponding byte in IP address is for the host id. So in other words 190.1.2 are for network id and 0,64,128 and 192 are for hosts. The last byte has eight bits, the first two bits are used to partition the hosts into 4 groups and the rest 6 bits are for identifying the individual hosts in each group.

190.1.2. 00 000000 to 190.1.2.00 111111 are for interface S1

190.1.2. 01 000000 to 190.1.2.01 111111 are for interface S2

190.1.2. 10 000000 to 190.1.2.10 111111 are for interface S3

190.1.2. 11 000000 to 190.1.2.11 111111 are for interface S4

Converting the last byte binary into decimal gives

190.1.2.0 to 190.1.2.63 for interface S1

190.1.2.64 to 190.1.2.127 for interface S2

190.1.2.128 to 190.1.2.191 for interface S3

190.1.2.192 to 190.1.2.255 for interface S4

Which means if a packet with destination IP address comes and is

a) following in the range of 190.1.2.0 to 190.1.2.63 will be directed to interface S1

b) following in the range of 190.1.2.64 to 190.1.2.127 will be directed to interface S2

c) following in the range of 190.1.2.128 to 190.1.2.191 will be directed to interface S3

d) following in the range of 190.1.2.192 to 190.1.2.255 will be directed to interface S4

g) Gateway

The activity of a gateway is much more complex than a router or a switch. The gateway is a node which acts as an entrance for other nodes in a network. The gateway has the ability to connect different networks which may or may not be using the same protocol such TCP/IP. If the connecting networks are not using the same protocol then it converts one to the other for smooth functioning. Routers work with same type of protocols and gateway work with different protocols. Gateways operate at network layer of OSI model. When a network wants to communicate with devices outside its boundary, then we use gateway. All networks have edges, the gateways are put on these edges. Any transmission in or out of the network must pass through the gateway.

h) Modem

A modem is an networking device that converts analog signal to digital signal and digital signal to analog signal. It is placed between the computer system and the internet. A dial -up modem connects your computer to the internet through a Internet Service Provider. A wireless modem uses radio frequencies to transmit data to and fro. A DSL (digital subscriber line) modem uses telephone lines to transmit data. The word modem comes from mo (modulator) + dem (demodulator). A router first lets the computing devices connect to the modem, which then lets them communicate with the rest of the world.

1.6 Data Representation

The data which is to be transmitted comes in the form of texts, numbers, images, audios and videos. The text consists of alphabets, numbers and symbols which are represented as bit patterns in ASCII or EBCDIC form.

ASCII (American Standard Code for Information Interchange) is a 7 bit representation for each symbol. Extended ASCII uses 8 bit representation to represent each symbol. Unicode uses 16 bits to represent and can represents a maximum of upto 65536 symbols.

Images are represented by bit patterns and are divided into a maximum of pixels. Each pixel is a small dot and each pixel is assigned a bit pattern.

Audio is continuous and is not discrete. Video may either be represented as continuous or it may be a combination of images.

1.7 Direction of Data Flow

When two devices communicate then they may use one of the following methods:

1) Simplex

2) Half-Duplex

3) Full-Duplex

<u>Simplex</u>

Here only one device is sending data and the other is only receiving it. So we say the communication is unidirectional. Eg keyboard. The Keyboard can only be used for taking input.

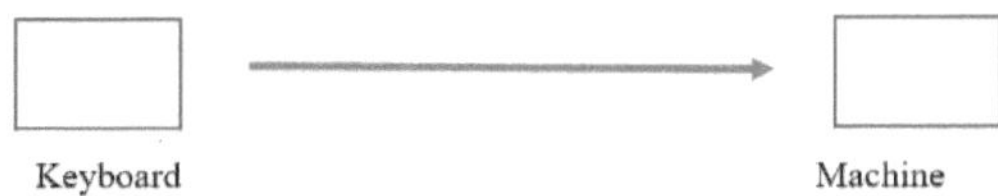

<u>Half-Duplex</u>

Here both the devices are capable of transmitting and both are capable of receiving also. But only one device can transmit at a single point of time. E,g Walkie -Talkie, One speaks at one time.

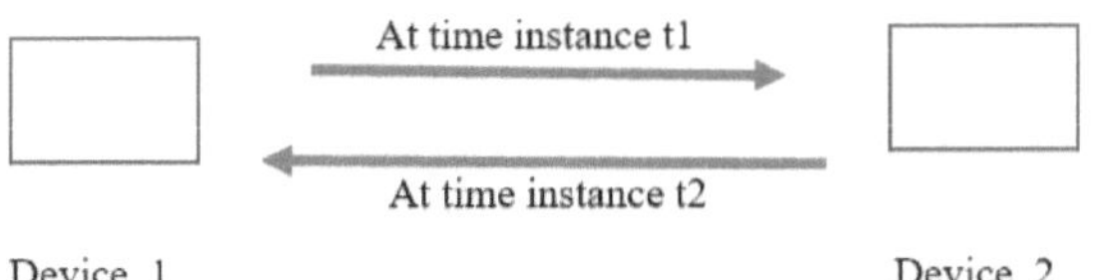

<u>Full Duplex</u>

Both Stations can transmit and receive. And can do at the same time or simultaneously. Eg,

Telephone , both can speak at the same time.

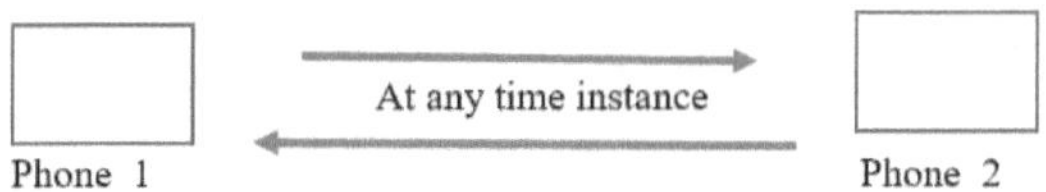

1.8 Types of Networks

The types of networks are based on the geographical area covered by them. They are as follows:

1) Local Area Network (LAN)

2) Metropolitan Area Network (MAN)

3) Wide Area Network (WAN)

4) Personal Area Network (PAN)

LAN

LAN is generally used to connect computers within a building or a home. It helps to share files or h/w among multiple users connected to it. The size of LAN is limited to a few hundred meters. It supports speed from 10Mbps to 10Gbps. A single cable is enough to do all the wiring. LAN can either be connected in a wired mode or in a wireless mode. Wired mode consists of Twisted Pair, Co-axial cable or fibre optic cable. LAN uses a set of protocol or rules to follow. It is less costly when compared to MANs or WANs. The hosts are linked in a particular topology such as Bus, Ring or Star.

LANs are of 3 types:

1) Cable based

2) Private Branch Exchange

3) Hierarchical Method

Cable based are such as co-axial cable or optic fiber. Private Branch Exchange is like a telephone network. Hierarchical is based on both cable based and Private Branch Exchange.

Advantages of LAN

1) It has high speed

2) It has little cost

3) Security can be implemented properly

4) Supports Email

5) Can share resources

Disadvantages of LAN

1) Expensive to install

2) Requires Administration time

3) Failure of File server can occur

4) Cable can break

MAN

MAN spreads around a whole city or a large campus such as a university campus. The geographical area of a MAN is more than that of a LAN. The owner of a MAN is a single organization but it can be used by many organizations. A MAN is a high speed network that can share resources. The area covered ranges from 5 KM to 50 KM. Example is a telephone network company servicing its customers through a high speed DSL.

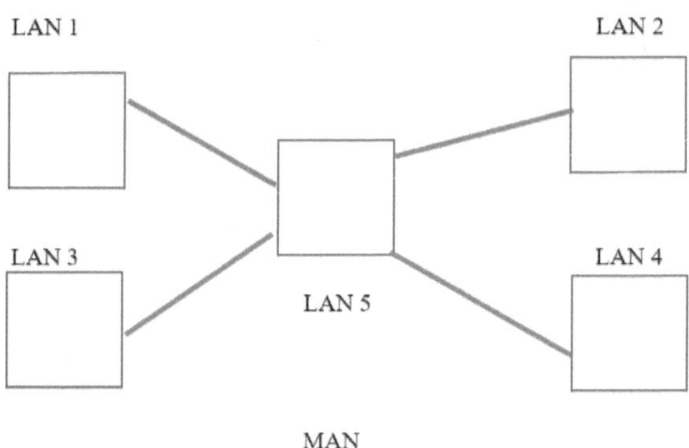

WAN

WAN covers a country, continent or the entire world. A WAN consists of 2 or more LANs or MANs connected together. The larger distances are covered by transmitting data over high speed telephone line or wireless links such as satellites. The multiple LANs can be connected through the devices such as bridges, routers or gateways which enable them to share data among other nodes. The example of a WAN is the internet.

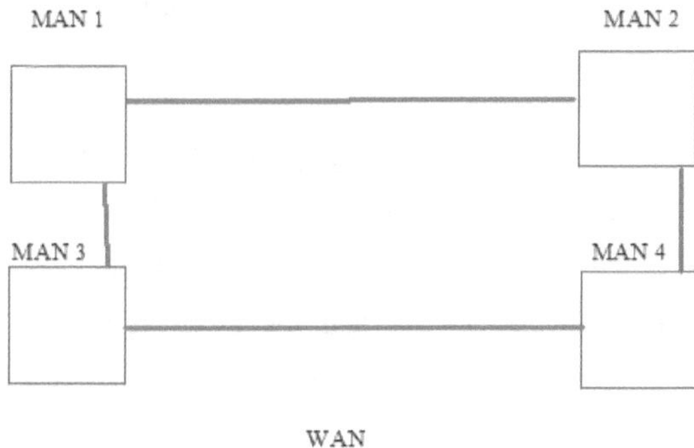

PAN

A PAN covers an area of a size of a room, ie a few meters. The devices connect among themselves or connect to a larger network such as an internet. PAN can be wired or wireless.

Eg. , a mobile in a room connected to a laptop, which is connected to the desktop, and to another Bluetooth device.

1.9 Topologies

Topologies refer to the layout of connected devices or a network. The logical layout of devices can be in any form such as follows:

1) Mesh

2) Star

3) Bus

4) Ring

5) Tree

6) Hybrid

MESH

Every device is connected to every other device in a point to point manner. Every node 1 is connected to every other n-1 nodes. To link the devices, the physical cables have to be of the order of n(n-1)/2. The number of ports should be (n-1) I/O ports.

Advantages of Mesh

1) There are dedicated links for each pair of nodes, so data transfer is through that link only. This eliminates the traffic problem

2) It is Robust which means if 1 link fails then other links are not affected by it.

3) Privacy and security is achieved because the links are dedicated.

4) The faults can be identified easily and can be isolated easily so that other nodes do not suffer.

Disadvantages of Mesh

1) The number of cables required is huge.

2) Number of I/O ports required is also large.

3) The bulk wiring takes up a large amount of space.

4) The h/w required for connecting is very exensive.

Example includes telephone network of a regional office.

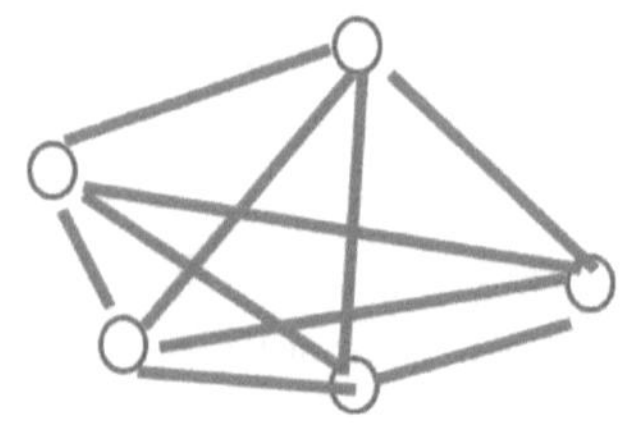

STAR

A central controller called a hub has a point to point dedicated link to each device. The traffic is not direct between 2 devices. All traffic goes through a central hub. If node 1 wants to send data to node 2, then node 1 sends data to the central hub and the central hub then passes data to node2.

Advantages of Star

1) Less costly when compared to Mesh because devices connect through the central hub.

2) Easy configuration and Installation capacity

3) If 1 node fails, all others are active

4) Cabling cost is less

5) Faults can be identified easily

6) When connecting or removing nodes, then other nodes are not disrupted.

Disadvantages of Star

1) The cabling is less than a mesh, but is much more than bus or ring topology

2) If the central hub is down, then whole network fails.

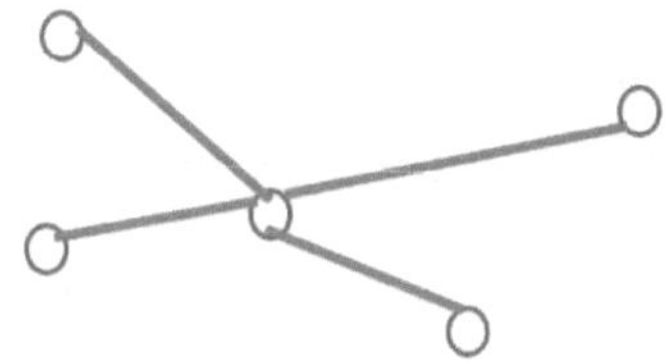

BUS

A bus is a multipoint network which means many devices can be connected to a single cable. Here a long cable acts as a backbone to which all devices connect. Only one device transmits at one time. If a device wants to send data to another device, it broadcast the message onto the cable. All devices receive it, but only the intended device accepts the message and processes it while all other devices discard the message as it was not meant for them.

Advantages of Bus

1) It is easy to install

2) It requires less cabling

<u>Disadvantages of Bus</u>

1) It is difficult to reconfigure

2) Isolation of faults is also difficult

3) To add new devices is also difficult

4) Travelling signals degrade over distances

5) If there is a fault in the backbone then whole network suffers

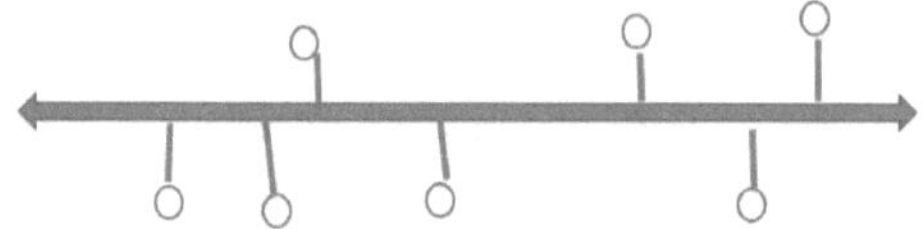

RING

Each device has 2 connections, one on its right hand side and the other on its left hand side. Each device has a repeater which passes the signal from one device to another until the intended device gets the message. On adding or removing a device only two connections need to be changed.

<u>Advantages of Ring</u>

1) Easy to install

2) Easy to configure

3) The identification of faults can be done easily.

<u>Disadvantages of Ring</u>

1) Message travels only in 1 direction

2) If there is a break in the ring, then whole network suffers

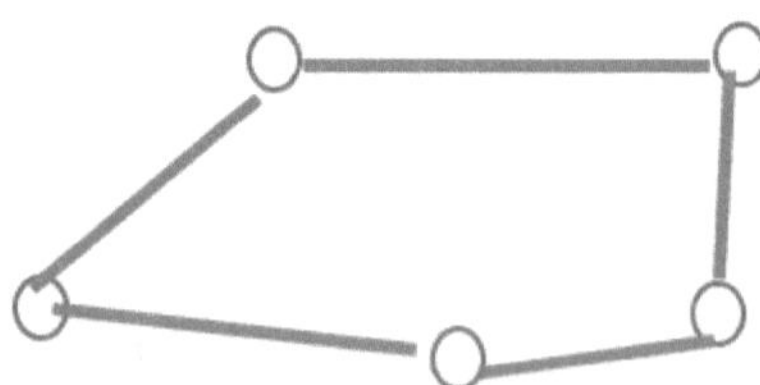

TREE

Tree is also known as star bus topology. A tree connects multiple star networks to other star networks.

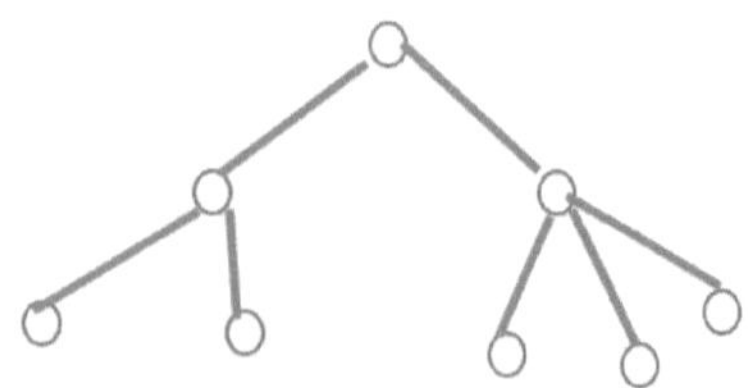

<u>**HYBRID**</u>

All topologies can connect to all other topologies on a single backbone.

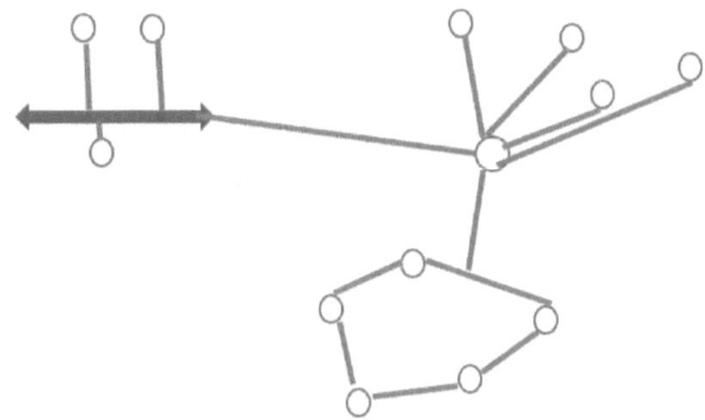

1.10 OSI Model and TCP/IP Model

OSI stands for Open Systems Interconnection and was developed by International Organization for Standardization (ISO) to describe the layered approach for networking.

<u>Layer</u>

Each layer provided services to the next higher layer and insulated the details of the lower layer from the upper layer. Each layer on the destination machine appeared to be communicating with its corresponding layer on the source machine. On source machine the communication moved down through the layer over to the destination machine where the communication moved up through the layers. Each layer added its own information to the message received from the upper layer and then passed the whole message to the layer down beneath it.

The purpose of the OSI model was to develop a framework so that protocols could be developed. IN OSI there are seven layers:

1) Physical Layer

2) Data Link Layer

3) Network layer

4) Transport Layer

5) Session Layer

6) Presentation Layer

7) Application Layer

Sends	Layer
Data	Application
Data	Presentation
Data	Session

Segments	Transport
Packets	Network
Frames	Data Link
Bits	Physical

The Physical Layer

The bit stream is transferred over a physical medium in this layer. The mechanical and electrical specifications are taken care of in this layer. Mechanical devices such as cable, plugs and pins and electrical considerations such as modulation, signal strength and voltage level. It defines the functions and procedures that physical devices have to perform in order to transmit.

The bits are encoded into electrical and optical signal to show how 0s and 1s are changed into signals. It also defines the rate at which bits will travel. The sender and receiver need to synchronize at the bit level. Information flows from top to bottom at the sender side and bottom to up at receiver side.

The Data Link Layer

This layer is responsible for node to node or hop to hop delivery. It makes the physical layer appear error free to the network layer. The functions of the link layer are:

1) Framing: The stream of bits received from the network layer are divided into manageable units called frames.

2) Physical Addressing: The frames are meant for particular machine therefore they are delivered to the particular machine by adding header to the frame to identify the sender and receiver of the frame.

3) Flow Control: If the rate at which the sender is sending is more than the rate at which receive is receiving then an overflow will occur which is taken care of by this layer.

4) Error Control: This is achieved by detecting and retransmitting lost or damaged frames. The duplication of frames need to be prevented. This is taken care of by adding trailer to the frame.

5) Access Control: When more than 1 device is connected to the same link, then which device has the access over the channel needs to be pointed out.

The Network Layer

Across the multiple networks, this layer is responsible for the delivery of the packets from the source machine to destination machine. It ensures that the packets given by the sender reach their destination. Each packet is treated as an independent packet. The functions of this layer are:

1) Logical Addressing: It sends the packet to and from the logical addresses of the receiver and sender. Here internetworking takes place by the packet taking an independent route to deliver from source to final destination.

The Transport Layer

This layer is responsible for process to process delivery. Its functions are:

1) Service Addressing : Here port numbers are used to identify a particular service at a particular machine. The process of 1machine connects to the process of the destination machine with the help of port numbers.

2) Segmentation and reassembly: The large message is divided into segments and each segment has a sequence number. The message arrives out of order so they need to reassemble. And if a packet is lost in the transmission, then it needs to be identified and replaced by retransmitting the packet.

3) Connection Control: This control may be connection oriented or connectionless. A connectionless control treats each packet independently and delivers to the destination. A connection oriented makes a connection between sender and receiver for transmitting.

4) Flow Control: performs end to end delivery.

5) Error Control: This is achieved through retransmission where the entire packet is delivered error free.

The Session Layer

It is used to establish, maintain and synchronize the interaction between connecting systems.

Its Functions are:

1) Dialog Control: Two system enter into a dialog. Communication may be half-duplex or full-duplex.

2) Synchronization: Checkpoints are added to the stream of data. Suppose after every 50th page a checkpoint is added. So it can be verified that those 50 pages arrived correctly.

The Presentation Layer

This layer takes care of the syntax and semantics of the data. Its functions are:

1) Translation: Different systems may use different ways to represent data. Suppose 1 machine uses the ASCII code for representing the data and another machine uses EBCDIC. Then they both need to agree on a common format and translate where necessary.

2) Encryption: Here sender need to convert plain text into cipher text and receiver needs to decrypt the cipher text back into plain text.

3) Compression: It reduces the number of bits for transmission.

The Application Layer

This layer deals with Electronic Mail, File transfer, directory services and remote login. A Network Virtual Terminal helps to login into a remote host. Files can be accessed and received from remote host. Email can be forwarded and stored. Distributed database sources can access global information.

TCP/IP MODEL

The OSI model was not successful because the presentation layer and session layer not able to perform their tasks and could not be implemented. The TCP/IP model was successful because it could be implemented properly. The Layers in this model are:

1) Application Layer

2) Transport Layer

3) Network Layer

4) Data Link Layer

5) Physical Layer

The Application Layer

This includes File transfer, Email, Remote Login etc. Its functions are:

1) Identifying communication partners

2) Determining resource availability

3) Synchronizing communication

4) Users can log into remote hosts

5) Various email services can be provided

6) Distributed database sources can be accessed to provide global information.

The Transport Layer

In this layer process on one machine can connect to process on another machine. Its functions are :

1) The rate of data sent can be controlled

2) Ensures that the data is error free and in sequence.

3) It provides segmentation and de segmentation.

4) To give acknowledgements of the data received

5) Divides message received from upper layer into segments and numbers them into a sequence.

6) Ensures message is delivered to the correct process on the destination machine.

7) If all message fails to be transmitted, it does so by retransmissions.

The Network Layer

Packets are sent from one network to another. They may take different routes to reach the destination. Variable length packets may travel from one node to another. It does not guarantee that the packets will be delivered but it does its best to do so.

The Data Link Layer

It gives the details as how data should be sent over the network. It defines how bits should be signaled over coaxial, twisted pair or optical fibers. How data transmission is done physically on the network. How data is sent between the two devices on the same network.

Advantages of TCP/IP

- Connection can be set up between different computers
- It is not dependent on the operating system used for operating
- It supports many routing-protocols.
- Organizations can perform internetworking
- It can scale up to higher levels with the client server architecture

Disadvantages of TCP/IP

- The set up and management of TCP/IP is difficult.
- IPX (Internetwork Packet Exchange) has lower overhead than TCP/IP
- Protocol replacement in TCP/IP is not easy
- The separation of Interfaces, Protocols and services is not distinct.

1.11 Connectionless and Connection Oriented service

In a connection oriented service, the clients and the servers send control messages to each other, before sending the actual data. The control messages perform a handshake which lets the client and the server know that they both are ready to transmit and receive packets.

The routers and links in between serve the purpose of transmitting the packets to the end systems. The end systems are aware that such a connection exists, other routers and in between devices are not aware of the connection and they do not maintain any connection state information.

The connection oriented service ensures reliability, which can be taken care of by acknowledgements and retransmissions. Suppose machine A is sending a message to machine B. If B receives the message from A, it sends an acknowledgement back to A. If B has not received any message from A, it will not send the acknowledgement and then A will retransmit the frame.

Apart from reliability, the connection oriented service also allows flow control and congestion control. Flow control means that if too many packets are sent at the same time and the receiver is not able to process them, then buffers are used to ensure that packets are not dropped.

If a router becomes too busy, and starts dropping packets, then this is known as congestion control and is taken care by sending packets through alternative route (through other routers). The most common protocol used by connection oriented service is TCP (Transmission Control Protocol).

In Connectionless service, there is no prior handshake between the sender and the receiver. The source simply keeps sending the packets without knowing whether they have reached the destination or not.

Also there in no protocol used for flow control or error control. The most common protocol used by connectionless service is UDP (User Datagram Protocol).

1.12 Packet Switching and Circuit Switching

In a network there are end systems connected with routers, switches and link transmissions. When one end systems wants to send any information to another end system, Then if the path that has been assigned to transfer packet from source to destination is reserved, then it is called Circuit Switching. In this scheme, all the components used to build this circuit are sending only those packets which have been assigned between the end systems. Packets other than the ones assigned are not allowed to use this reserved path.

In packet switching, the path is not reserved. If a packet has to transfer from source to destination, then it may travel a certain path. If the 2nd packet of the same communication is sent, then it may take a different route from source to destination. The resources are made available as per the traffic in the network. If one path is having lot of traffic on it, then the packet takes an alternate path.

The example of circuit switching is the telephone network and the connection reserved for it is called the circuit.

In packet switching there is no bandwidth reserved and the User Datagram Protocol provides best delivery effort. Best delivery means it tries its best possible to deliver the packet, but it cannot guarantee that the packet will be received by the receiver. If it is lost in between transmission then, the source does not do anything.

In circuit switching, an end to end connection is established between 2 hosts. For a message to go from host A to host B, one circuit on each of the 2 links gets reserved.

<u>Circuit Switching Multiplexing</u>

There are 3 ways in which a circuit switched network can be multiplexed.

1) Frequency Division Multiplexing

2) Time Division Multiplexing

3) Code Division Multiplexing

In Frequency Division Multiplexing, the band of frequency is shared among participating entities. Each participating entity gets a dedicated band to transmit its packet. Generally between 88MHz to 108MHz.

The time is divided into a number of frames, one frame consists of 4 subparts, each subpart is known as a slot. The frames are sent onto the link one after another. Each connection is allocated a slot number. Say if you wish to transfer packets from machine A to machine B, then let the slot allotted to this connection be 1. Which means whenever the time comes of slot 1, packets will be sent from A to B. Suppose there is another connection from Machine C to Machine D and the slot allocated to this connection is 2. Whenever the time slot 2 comes, it will transfer packets from C to D.

TDM

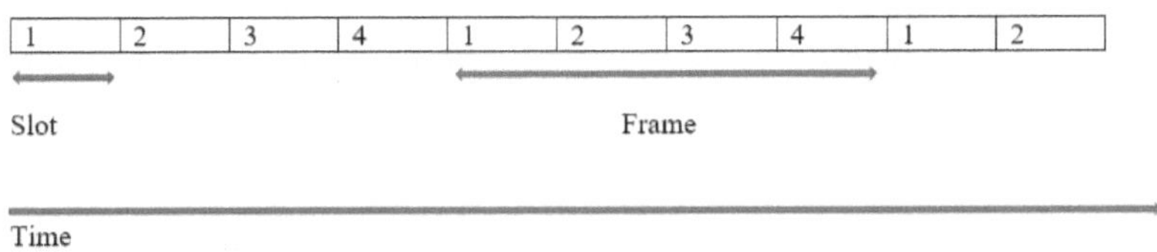

CDM

In Code Division Multiple Access (CDMA), All stations are able to transmit data at the same time. The data is transmitted over the entire frequency range at all times. These multiple simultaneous transmissions are distinguished on the basis of unique code sequences. Every user has his own code sequence and they are generated by using a set of orthogonal vectors.

<u>Packet Switching</u>

When large amount of data has to be transmitted across the network, then it is broken down into smaller chunks of data known as packets. Between the source and destination, there are routers and switches attached to facilitate the transmission. These routers and switches are known as packet switches which use the store and forward transmission mechanism to deliver the packets. The routers or the packet switches have multiple links attached to it. Each attached link has a buffer, so that packets arriving at it can be buffered. If a packet arrives at the link and finds that the router is too busy sending other packets then it waits and is put in a queue which is known as output queue or output buffer. This introduces queuing delays.

Now the buffer space is also limited, suppose router is busy sending packets and its output queue is also full. Then in that case the router will drop packets and this is known as packet loss. It may drop either the arriving packets or one of the already queued packets will be dropped.

<u>Packet Switched Networks</u>

There are 2 types of packet switched networks:

    1) Datagram Networks

    2) Virtual Circuit Networks

The difference between the 2 is based on how to interpret the destination address.

If the packet is forwarded by looking at the host destination address, then that is called a datagram network. Now if the packet is forwarded by looking at the virtual circuit numbers, then it is called Virtual Circuit Network.

<u>Virtual Circuit Network</u>

The Virtual Circuit is made by 2 connecting end systems and the routers and switches used in between to deliver the packet from source to destination. When a virtual circuit is established, it is given a virtual circuit id or VCID. The packet switches have a table that tells which VCID needs to go to which outbound link. When a packet arrives, the VCID table is examined and packet forwarded to the outbound link. Whenever a new virtual circuit is established, it is given a new table entry in the packet switch's translation table.

<u>Datagram Network</u>

When a packet is received at the router, the router examines the destination address in the header of the packet. On checking the destination address, it decides to which outbound link does the packet need to go. For this purpose, the router maintains a forwarding table in which there are entries of network ids matched with the outbound link interface.

So the network id bytes of the destination address are looked up in the forwarding table and packets sent to adjacent outbound link.

The datagram network does not maintain connection state information in their routers. The forwarding decision is dependent on the packet's destination address, and not upon the connection to which the packet belongs.

In VC networks, the connection state information is installed and removed as per the connection is made or terminated respectively.

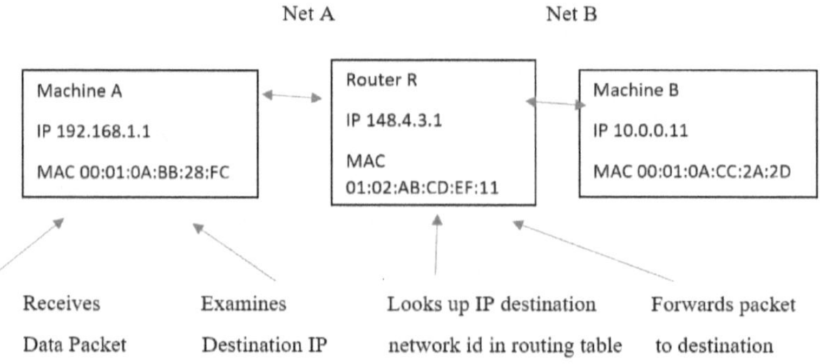

Source IP is Machine A 192.168.1.1

Destination IP is Machine B 10.0.0.11

Network A connected to router has IP address 192.168.1.0

Network B connected to router has IP address 10.0.0.0

10.0.0.11 is not on Network A's subnet, so it binds the MAC address of the Router as destination MAC address which is 01:02:AB:CD:EF:11.

The router's interface on network id receives the packet because the destination MAC address belongs to it. That network then throws away the header of the physical layer and is left with the IP layer which consists of Source IP address, Destination IP address and data.

Now the IP datagram inspects the destination IP field.

Network Name	Network Range
A	192.168.1.0/24
B	10.0.0.0/24

10.0.0.0 is on network B, so it transfers the packet to network B. The destination IP address is 10.0.0.11, which is machine B, and it is connected to network B. So the router now forms a packet and gives the destination MAC address of machine B, which is 00:01:0A:CC:2A:2D. And it keeps the source MAC address of its own, which is 01:02:AB:CD:EF:11

1.13 Media Access and Physical Medium

The packet at the lowest most layer transfers from one physical medium to another. The types are as follows:

1) Residential Access : The PCs at home are connected onto the network.

2) Company Access: The PCs in an organization may be connected on a network

3) Wireless Access: The physical medium is through WiFi. Signals are sent into the air and received on the other side.

<u>Residential Access</u>

Residential Access is done through a Dial-Up-Modem connected to the terminal and the Internet Service Provider (ISP). The digital output sent by the PC is converted into an analog signal which is sent over the telephone line. The ISP has another modem which converts the coming analog signal into a digital signal which is provided to the ISP router. The analog signal line of the telephone network is made up of twisted pair of copper wires.

New technologies have come into the market to provide broadband connections. This is known as DSL(Digital Subscriber Line). The DSL transmission rates are very high. DSL uses Frequency Division Multiplexing.

Company Access

An organization uses a Local Area Network (LAN) to connect to all the PCs in a building or so. This typically uses the Ethernet technology. The transmission rate of an Ethernet varies from 10 Mbps to 100 Mbps.

A twisted pair copper wire or coaxial cable is used to connect the system together with each other. An edge router is placed in a network and it is used to provide connectivity to other networks. The edge routers send packets outside of the LAN.

Wireless Access

The wireless access can be seen in mobile phones. The wireless access is divided into 2 categories:

1) Wireless LAN

2) Wide Area Wireless Access Network

In a wireless LAN, the users can send or receive packets from a node called the base station. The base station is also referred to as a Wireless Access Point, this runs through an area covering a few tens of meters. The base station is connected to a wired network, therefore it is a point where the wired medium meets the wireless medium.

Physical Medium

The physical medium may consist of twisted pair cable or a fibre optic cable. The Physical medium transmits bits across from sender to receiver. Physical medium is of two types:

1) Guided Medium

2) Unguided Medium

Guided Medium includes transmission through solid medium such as:

1) Fibre Optic

2) Twisted pair Cable

3) Coaxial Cable

The Unguided Media has waves which are sent in the air, they are of two types:

1) Wireless LAN

2) Digital Satellite Channel

Twisted Pair Copper Wire

These are insulated copper wires arranged in a spiral pattern of 1mm thickness. The twisted nature helps to prevent interference from closely placed other twisted pair wires.

Coaxial Cable

The Coaxial Cable has 2 conductors which are placed concentric to each other rather than parallel. This is mostly used in cable TV sets. It has speed of 1 Mbps or higher. A number of systems can be used to share data with the help of shared medium. All end systems are connected to the shared cable.

Fibre Optic

A thin optical fibre transfers pulses of light. Each pulse represents a single bit. The transmission rate is nearly equal to hundreds of gigabytes per second. The electromagnetic interference do not hamper the transmissions as they are immune to it. These fibres are used to transmit over wide ranges such as overseas transmissions.

Wireless LAN

This technology uses radio channels which are easily passed through buildings, walls and can also operate if the user is moving. They are used for long distances. The signals might fail if there is loss of path, or they may loose their strength after travelling large distances. Also if there is interference from other signals, then the signal can experience low quality transmission. These increase productivity and provide convenience. Packets are sent via radio waves. The packets contain MAC addresses which enable them to be delivered at the intended end point. A WAN can be set up in two ways:

1) Infrastructure

2) Ad hoc

In the Infrastructure mode which is like setting up a WAN at home, all end points communicate with the help of a base station. A wireless router functions as a base station and end points mean all computing devices such as printer, mobile devices, computers etc.

In Ad hoc mode, the computers and end points are not connected to the base station. A Wi-Fi direct technology is used for setting up the connections. These provide peer to peer (P2P) communication. After adjusting their network settings the devices are able to communicate with each other.

Bluetooth

Many devices are connected together to each other through radio frequency replacing the wired connections. Some examples are Headset for mobile phones allow you to talk while the mobile phone is placed at some distance, speakers for car stereos are paired with each other, Television is paired with remote controls.

Bluetooth technology is used for connecting smaller devices such as speaker to tablet. It can perform the same function of a WiFi and cellular phones but it leaves that responsibility with larger network connecting devices to the internet.

Bluetooth works on the master slave technology. One master is connected to many slaves forming a piconet. One master can be connected to at most 7 slaves, whereas one slave canbe connected to only a single master.

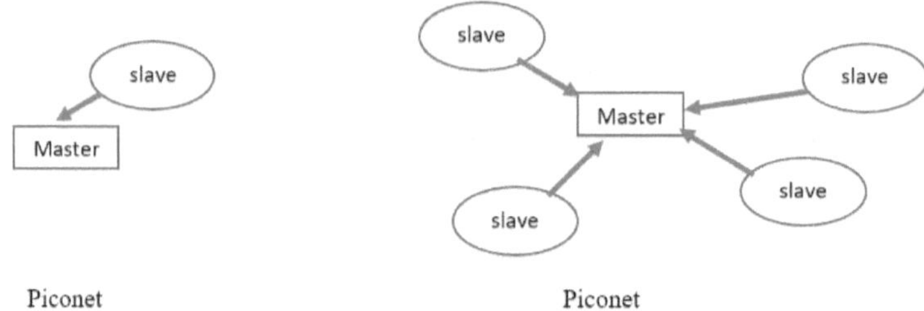

The slaves can only talk to the master that they are connected to. They cannot talk to each other directly. The master can send data to them and collect data from them.

Every Bluetooth device has a 48 bit address which is given as a 12 digit hexadecimal value. The most significant 24 bits of the hexadecimal are given by the manufacturer which is used as an identification of the organization or network. The least significant 24 bits of the hexadecimal specify the unique ID of the devices.

Example,

If we have a 12 bit hexadecimal address as 877884566812, then

877884 is the organization address and

566812 is the address of the device

<u>Broadband Wireless</u>

Wireless Broadband provides its services through a Wireless Local Area Network (WLAN) or through a Wireless Wide Area Network(WWAN). The term broadband signifies that the delivery will be high speed upto at least 25 Mega bits per second (Mbps). To implement wireless broadband needs a router or a modem which can connect from the user's home to the Internet Service Provider (ISP). The transmission of radio waves take place when connected.

The wireless broadband is divided into 2 categories:

1) Fixed Wireless Broadband

2) Mobile Wireless Broadband

In fixed wireless broadband, the router etc are fixed in one spot, be it an office or a user at home. The key point is that instead of copper wires, radio waves are used.

In Mobile Wireless Broadband, the high speed internet is provided to mobile devices which are randomly located, for example the cellular wireless broadband.

In cellular wireless broadband, the internet is provided by the cellular network provider. They use base stations to send and receive data. The data is transmitted directly to the mobile phone of the user.

<u>Satellite Radio Channel</u>

A satellite receives transmissions on one frequency band and transmits the signal to another frequency band. The satellites are capable of providing transmission rate equal to gigabit per second.

Ground stations are linked to one another through the satellite. These ground stations receive or transmit microwaves. Satellites are of two types:

    1) Geo Stationary Satellites

    2) Low Altitude Satellites

Geo Stationary satellites are placed at a single position above the earth and they move at the same speed as the earth. Low Altitude satellites are not placed at a single point above the earth. They are placed much closer to the earth and they revolve around the earth just as the moon does and cover the area of the earth they are passing through.

1.14 Delay and Loss in Packet Switched Networks

In a packet switched network, the message is passed from source to destination via routers, switches, gateways etc. This process takes time and may face delay and loss of packets. There are a number of delays associated with it and they are as follows:

    1) Processing Delay

    2) Queuing Delay

    3) Transmission delay

    4) Propagation Delay

<u>Processing Delay</u>

This delay occurs because time is required to check the header's contents and find out where the packet should be forwarded. Also bit error checking is done during this time. The packet is then forwarded to the appropriate queue.

<u>Queuing Delay</u>

This occurs when the packet is waiting in a queue ready to be transmitted. This delay is caused by a number of already waiting packets in the queue. If the queue is empty, the packet will quickly go through. If lots of packets are waiting, then this delay takes place.

<u>Transmission Delay</u>

The packets are generally sent on First Come First Serve basis. Suppose the length of the packet is L bits and the rate of transmission is R bits per second. Then the transmission is L/R. The transmission rate R is given beforehand. If the transmission rate of Ethernet uses 10Mbps, then R will be 10Mbps. If the transmission rate of Ethernet is 100Mbps, then R will be 100Mbps.

Example

Suppose the rate of transmission is 5Mbps(R) and size of the packet is 1500 bits (L), then the transmission delay is L/R

$= 1500 / 5 \times 10^6$

$= 3 \times 10^{-4}$ seconds

$= 0.3$ miliseconds

<u>Propagation Delay</u>

This is the time taken by the packet to move from source to destination. The bits propagate at the propagation speed of the link. This propagation time depends upon the physical medium. For example, optic fibre takes less time to propagate than the twisted pair cable. The propagation delay is defined as the distance between two routers divided by the propagation speed.

Propagation Delay = d/s

Where d is the distance

And s is the speed.

The speed of light is 3×10^8 m/s

The speed through the optic fibre is 2.1×10^8 m/s

Suppose we have a two machine which are 3000 meters apart and travel through optic fibre, then the propogation delay will be given by

$= 3000/2.1 \times 10^8$

$= 1.428 \times 10^{-5}$ seconds

$= 0.01428$ miliseconds

The total delay at a node is given by

d_total = d_processing + d_queuing + d_transmission + d_propagation

<u>Packet Loss</u>

Packet loss happens when the queue is full and cannot accommodate any more packets, then the system starts dropping the packets. If there is an ideal system in which no queueing delay is there, then the end to end delay will occur.

d_end_to_end = d_processing + d_transmission + d_propagation

1.15 Layered Architecture

Application layer runs well known services like HTTP(Hyper Text Transfer Protocol) and FTP (File Transfer Protocol). It is also able to handle applications which are not well known but built for a specific purpose. Those services are also running at some port number. So applications running on a machine are distinguished by port numbers.

Transport Layer runs Services such as UDP and TCP. Where UDP is connectionless service and TCP is connection oriented.

Internet Protocol layer is used to identify the machine on which the datagram is to be sent. All machines on the internet are identified by Internet Protocol addresses which are more commonly known as IP addresses.

The data link layer deals with the MAC addresses, which is Media Access Control addresses. These addresses are given by the manufacturer at the time of making the computer system. They are inscribed on NIC (Network Interface Card). The MAC addresses and IP addresses are mapped to each other for the identification of a machine.

MAC addresses are used to identify the machine at the data link layer level and IP addresses are used to identify the machine at the IP layer level. Both of them are equally important to identify a machine and have their unique role.

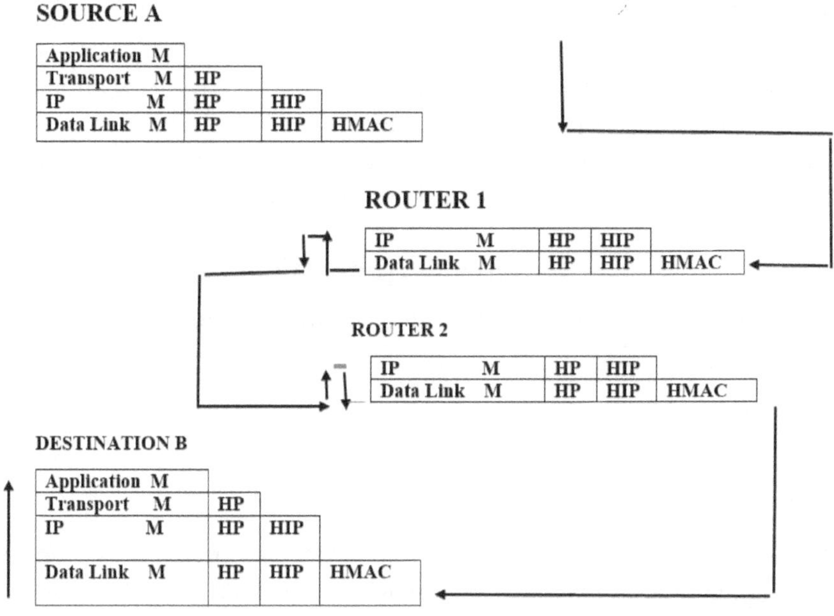

At the source A, there is a message M that needs to be transported to destination B. At source A, The message M travels down to the transport layer which adds the source port number and destination port number as the header HP. It further passes down to the IP layer which carries the above message as it is and further adds the source IP address and the destination IP address as the header HIP. It further passes down to the data link layer which adds the source MAC address and the destination MAC address as the header HMAC.

Now we have a complete frame which travels through the physical medium to the Router 1. The Router 1 sheds the HMAC header which contains the source MAC address of Source A and destination MAC address of itself and passes the rest of the fragment to its upper layer, which is the IP layer. The IP layer of Router 1 inspects the IP header HIP which contains the Source IP address of source A and destination IP address of destination B. On examining, it finds that the destination address will be reached, if packet is forwarded to Router 2. So the router 1 adds the HMAC, which contains it own MAC address as the Source MAC address and the destination MAC as that of the router 2. Router 2 on receiving the frame again sheds the MAC address which is HMAC and passes the packet to its upper layer which is IP layer of router 2. It inspects the destination IP address fields and sees that the packet is meant for destination B, which is on the same network as the router 2 itself. So it adds the HMAC header which now contains the source MAC address as of itself and the destination MAC address of the Destination B and it passes the packet in the network. Destination B receives the packet as it has B's destination address. B sheds HMAC header and passes to its upper layer, which is IP layer. IP layer sees the header HIP, it contains the IP address of B, so it sheds the header HIP and passes the rest to its upper layer, which is the transport layer. Transport layer inspects the header HP, which contains the soured port number and the destination port number. It sheds the header HP and passes the message to the application which is running on the port number given by the destination port number.

1.16 Network Applications

There are 3 main architectures that deal with network applications, they are:

    1) Client Server Architecture

    2) Peer to Peer Architecture (P2P)

    3) Hybrid of P2P and client server

<u>Client Server Architecture</u>

There are a number of hosts called the clients which connect to a single server. The server is continuously running in the background. Each client connects to it and passes its request. The clients do not directly connect to each other. The server has a fixed IP address whereas all clients have their unique IP addresses. The clients can be put off whereas the server must be up all the time. The server takes the responsibility of serving the client requests without losing any one of these.

<u>Peer to Peer Architecture (P2P)</u>

There is no server in this architecture, only peers known as clients communicate with each other. There is no hard restriction that the clients have to be on all the time.If one client dies after completing its work, then when it comes back again, it may have a different IP address than what it had in the previous transaction. The advantage of P2P architecture is that lots of computers can be added and increased at run time without having any hassles of a server.

<u>Hybrid of P2P and client server</u>

Here a server exists but it does not require to be on all the time. The P2P facility can be achieved by 2 clients when they want to chat with each other, they need not connect to the server, they can communicate directly. The server is required if a new system comes into existence and wants to register itself. When one client wants to know all other peers who are currently logged in, then the server can be contacted to find that out.

1.17 The Communicating Processes

A process is a program in execution. The processes of two different machines communicate with each other by sending/receiving packets into the network. These processes whether it is a client process or a server process, they run on their machines on different port numbers. Thus to communicate each process needs the IP address and the port number on which it is running.

The IP address and the port number pair is known as a socket.

HOST / CLIENT	SERVER
IP ADDRESS 148.6.8.1	IP ADDRESS 192.62.18.2
PORT NUMBER 60	PORT NUMBER 112

So the socket at host or client is given by { 148.6.8.1 : 60}

And socket at server is given by { 192.62.18.2 :112}

Thus it means that the Source IP address is 148.6.8.1 and Source port number is 60 (at which client application is running). The destination IP address is 192.62.18.2 and the destination port number is 112 (at which the server application is running, the one which client wants to interact with).

The following table shows the port numbers and by who all are they used.

Port Group	Port Numbers	Used By
Well Known Ports	0- 1023	Reserved for Common or popular services such as FTP, HTTP, TELNET
Registered Ports	1024 – 49151	Individual applications of users
Ephemeral Ports	49152 – 65535	When a connection to a service is initiated, this port no identifies the client application.

Port Number	Protocol	Application
20	TCP	File Transfer Protocol (FTP) - Data
21	TCP	File Transfer Protocol (FTP) - Control
22	TCP	Secure Shell (SSH)
23	TCP	Telnet
25	TCP	Simple Mail Transfer Protocol (SMTP)
53	UDP, TCP	Domain Name Service (DNS)
67	UDP	Dynamic Host Configuration Protocol (DHCP) - Server
68	UDP	Dynamic Host Configuration Protocol - Client
69	UDP	Trivial File Transfer Protocol (TFTP)
80	TCP	Hypertext Transfer Protocol (HTTP)
110	TCP	Post Office Protocol version 3 (POP3)
143	TCP	Internet Message Access Protocol (IMAP)
161	UDP	Simple Network Management Protocol (SNMP)
443	TCP	Hypertext Transfer Protocol Secure (HTTPS)

CHAPTER 2
THE APPLICATION LAYER

2.1 Introduction

The Application layer deals with the applications that the user writes in order to communicate with each other. The Applications may be widely used applications or the individual applications written by users.

Here is given a display of well known applications, which run on the well known protocols.

    1) Electronic Mail, runs on SMTP (Simple Mail Transfer Protocol)

    2) Remote Terminal Access, runs on Telnet (TeleNetworking)

    3) Web Service, runs on HTTP (Hyper Text Transfer Protocol)

    4) File Transfer, runs on FTP (File Transfer Protocol)

    5) Remote File Server runs on NFS (Network File System)

The Application Layer protocols run above the Transport Layer protocols. There are 2 types of transport layer protocols, UDP and TCP. UDP (User Datagram Protocol) and TCP (Transmission Control Protocol). UDP is connection less , whereas TCP is connection oriented.

Let us discuss each of the protocol in detail.

2.2 Hyper Text Transfer Protocol (HTTP)

The HTTP protocol serves to run the web services given by the World Wide Web(WWW). The HTTP protocol requires that there is a program running at the client site known as a client program and a program running at the server site known as the server program. The web page is made up of objects. The object may be of different types such as an HTML file, a JPEG image, a GIF file, an Audio or a Video clip.

Individual web pages are fetched by giving the URL of the page. The URL (Uniform Resource Locator) looks like this:

    http://www.newcollege.edu.in

The client site program can be mentioned as the web browser. The web browser can be of the type chrome or internet explorer. A client makes a request to the server by an HTTP request message. The server responds with an HTTP response message, which contains the objects.

If the underlying protocol beneath the HTTP is TCP, then a connection is made to the server before sending an HTTP request. Once the connection is established, both client and server use their sockets pairs to communicate.

A term Round Trip Time (RTT) is used to define the time that the packet takes to go from client to server and back from server to client including the propagation delay, processing delay and queuing delay. There are 2 types of delay that the RTT encounters, 1st is the time taken to establish the TCP connection and the 2nd is the request/ response of the object.

An HTTP request message consists of the following:

    1) Request Line

    2) Header Line

    3) Blank Line

    4) Entity Body

Request line has METHOD, URL and VERSION

METHOD is GET or POST

Version is Version of HTTP

The Entity Body contains the words that you are going to search. The server sees the contents in the body and serves accordingly.

<u>Web Caching</u>

The web cache is a proxy server which does the work of the original web server, and it has the data stored in its own storage capacity. The web cache works as a server and as a client also. When a different client sends it a request and it is able to process and respond back with the answer, it is working as a server, When it asks something from the original server, it makes a request to the server, it is working like a client.

The advantage of web cache is that it reduces the response time of the client requests something and this leads to reduction in terms of cost also.

2.3 File Transfer Protocol (FTP)

FTP is a file transfer protocol which connects the local host to the remote host, establishes a connection and can then further transfer/receive files from local host to remote host.

HTTP and FTP both run on top of the TCP protocol of the transport layer and therefore both of them require connection establishment. FTP is used in 2 types of connections:

    1) Control Connection

    2) Data Connection

In control connection, it gives userid and password to connect to the remote host. Once it is connected, it can "put" or "get" files in the data connection mode. FTP runs on well known port number 21 for control connection and runs on well known port number 20 for data connection.

A local host initiates a control connection to the server by sending its userid and password over the connection. The local host also sends a command to change the remote directory. The server side sees that two commands have come, one for the login and another for changing a directory. So it initiates a data connection from server to host. The FTP used here sends only 1 file over the connection, if another file has to be sent, the new data connection is formed. The control connection for the session remains the same, but new data connections are set up whenever there is a transfer of file.

Some common FTP commands are:

    1) USER <username>

    2) PASS <password>

    3) LIST – this asks the server to send the list of file available in the current directory of the remote host.

    4) RETR <filename> - this is used for retrieving the file from the current directory of the remote host

    5) STOR <filename> - this is used for putting the file in the current directory of the remote host

2.4 Electronic Mail

An Electronic mail is built keeping in mind that the user may not be able to receive the mail at the time it is sent. Therefore it goes in a queue called the inbox. People read mails when it is convenient to them, also there are attachments allowed with the message. So users can send photos, audio, video clips along with the text.

There are 3 major components in a mail system, they are:

    1) User Agents

    2) Mail Server

    3) SMTP (Simple Mail Transfer Protocol)

Each site has its own user agents and mail servers. A user agent is responsible for creating the mail component and forwards it to its mail server. The mail server uses SMTP to transfer the mail to the mail server of the recipient. When the recipient is ready to read the mail, its user agent gets the mail from its mail server and put it in a queue.

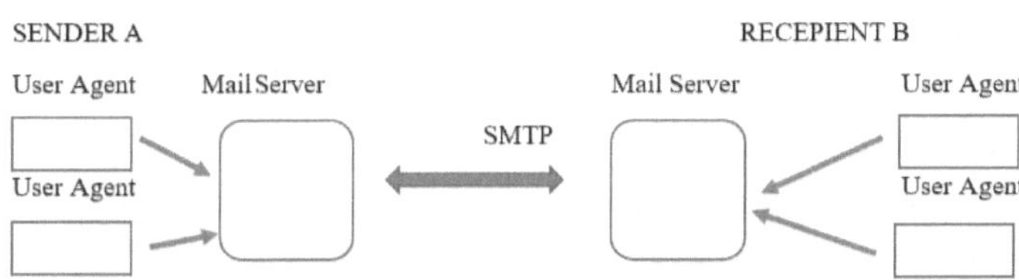

SMTP also works on top of TCP because TCP is reliable and UDP is not. These days mails have become important as they can be produced in court for documentary evidence. Therefore it works on a reliable transport layer protocol.

SMTP has two sides, a client side and a server side. All mail servers have both of the SMTP sides available for use. When a mail server passes the mail to another mail server, it works as an SMTP client. When a mail server receives a mail from another mail server, it works as an SMTP server.

The steps that take place in an SMTP transfer are as follows:

Here the sender is A and the receiver is B.

1) A invokes its user agent and constructs the mail message.

2) A's user agent sends the message to A's mail server and puts it in a queue.

3) The client side of SMTP sees that there is a message in the queue, so it opens a TCP connection with SMTP server of recipient B.

4) After handshaking, the message is put into the network.

5) At recipient B, the server side of SMTP receives the message and puts it in the mailbox of B.

6) When B is ready to read the message, its user agent gets to open the mail box and read the message.

2.5 Domain Name System (DNS)

A person can be identified by his name or his aadhar number. The name is given in alphabets and aadhar is given in integers. For a human it is easy to remember names than a series of numbers. That is why when a machine is identified uniquely it is done by IP addresses which is in numeric form such as 192.5.6.3.

If people want to reach to a particular machine, they would have to remember the IP addresses. To solve this problem, DNS was introduced which uniquely identifies a machine by names rather than IP addresses. There is direct mapping of machine names to IP addresses. The packets travel over the network by IP addresses, but when it comes to telling which machine is to be connected, we use the character based naming. The DNS runs over UDP protocol of the transport layer and is run on well known port number 53.

Protocols such as HTTP, SMTP and FTP use the DNS service to get their hostnames converted into IP addresses. For example, we want to run HTTP and want to connect to the machine www.newcollege.edu.in (hostname). The following steps take place:

1) The sender machine runs the client side of the DNS application.

2) The browser takes the hostname (www.newcollege.edu.in) given in the URL and passes the hostname to the client side of DNS application.

3) The DNS client makes a query containing the hostname and gives to the DNS server.

4) The server processes the hostname and makes a reply which contains the IP address for the corresponding hostname that was provided to it.

5) The DNS client receives the reply which has the IP addresses.

6) On receiving the IP addresses from DNS, a TCP connection is established by HTTP to the recipient machine.

It can be observed, that DNS would also take some time to reply, this adds on to the delay of HTTP. To solve this problem, we have a DNS server nearby which contains the IP addresses of the machine lying near it. With this we can reduce the DNS network traffic as well as the average DNS delay.

A few other functionalities are provided by the DNS along with translating to IP addresses:

1) Host Aliasing: A complicated hostname comes along with one or more alias names.

For example,www.news12.text.com may have alias as www.new12.com or new12.com. Here www.news12.text.com is known as canonical hostname.

2) Load Balancing: web servers are often replicated because they have lots of requests to be processed. Each web server runs on different end systems and has a different IP address. The replicated web server has a set of IP addresses associated with each canonical hostname. The DNS database contains these set of IP addresses associated with each web server. When a query is made for the named server, the entire list of IP addresses is provided as a reply. The difference is that those IP addresses are kept in circular mode. So whenever a new request comes, the IP addresses ae rotated.

A DNS server is distributed by nature. These are the reasons that we cannot have centralized DNS:

1) Failure of the centralized DNS causes the whole internet to fail.

2) If all requests are directed to the centralized DNS server then there would be a lot of traffic.

3) If the centralized DNS is placed at a large distance from the requesting machine, then it will cause significant delays.

4) The centralized DNS would contain all the records of the entire world. It will take a lot of time and effort to update the records.

Therefore the design of DNS is hierarchical and distributed.

The DNS servers are divided into 3 major categories, they are:

1) Root DNS Server

2) Top Level Domain DNS Server

3) Authoritative DNS Server

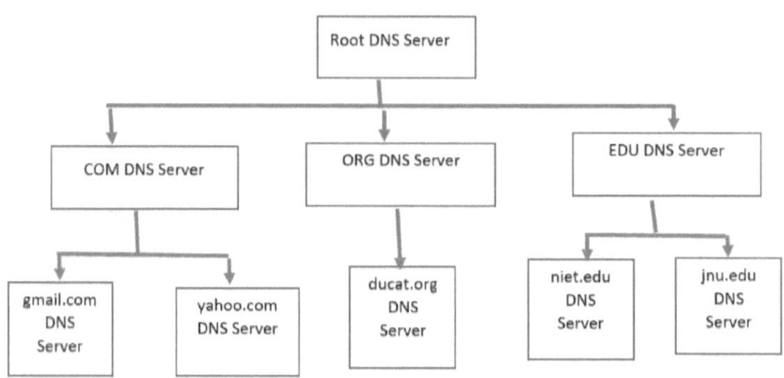

Suppose we want to determine the IP address for the hostname www.myntra. com. In this case the client contacts one of the root server, which returns the IP address for the top level domain .com . The client then makes a request to the top level domain server which return the address of the administrative server for myntra. com. This authoritative server then gives back the IP address of www.myntra.com.

Root level DNS server are replicated so that security and reliability can be provided. They are 13 in number worldwide. The top level domain servers are the ones ending in .org, .com, .edu, .net, .gov and also country codes such as .in, .au, .jp, .us, .uk, .fr. The authoritative domain within an organization can be implemented and changed by the organization itself. The records of these are kept in the authoritative DNS.

2.6 P2P File Sharing

P2P means peer to peer file sharing which includes that the peers (or hosts) can share video, audio, images, documents, s/w etc. Peer to Peer paradigm is based on client server architecture, the requesting peer is the client and the responding peer is the server. All the peers have the capability to run both client side and the server side of the file transfer protocol. There are a number peers available for transferring files, images, video, audios. Suppose the peer A wants to download a file, then that peer must find a way to determine the IP addresses of the connected peers which contain the desired file. As we know that peers connect and disconnect, so the problem is of considerable scale. There are 3 ways in which the problem can be solved;

1) Centralized based

2) Decentralized based

3) Hybrid of Centralized and Decentralized

<u>Centralized Directory</u>

A centralized directory uses a large server to provide the directory service. When a peer is ready, it informs the directory server of its IP addresses and the list of objects it has that can be shared. Then the directory server comes to know which objects are available for sharing. The directory server acts as a dynamic database that maps each object to a set of IP addresses. If a peer adds a new object or deletes an existing object, the directory server is informed accordingly so that updates can be made in the directory server. A peer can disconnect itself by closing the P2P client application or simply by disconnecting from the internet. Following are the disadvantages of using centralized directory:

1) If the directory server fails, the whole system will fail,

2) Lot of traffic in case of centralized server because thousands of queries in a single second have to be answered.

3) Reliability and performance issue is constrained because the transfer of contents over the network may be done in decentralized manner but locating which peers have the contents is centralized.

An example of this is Napster.

<u>Decentralized Approach</u>

In the decentralized approach we use a technique called Query Flooding. Query flooding is carried out to discover the contents in a decentralized manner. An example of this is Gnutella. In this the peers form an abstract, logical network known as Overlay Network. The overlay network is a graph which is made by connecting edges. An edge exists between A and B if there is a TCP connection between A and B. All active peers and connecting edges form the graph. In Gnutella, a peer has less than 10 connecting nodes.

A peer sends a message to its neighbouring peer which are connected by pre-existing TCP connection in the overlay network. Suppose A wants to find the file <hello>. It sends a query containing the word <hello> to all its neighbours. Those neighbours then forward the query to their neighbours, which in turn forward to their neighbours. This is the way in which query flooding takes place.

During the process, if a peer has the file <hello>, it will respond back to A giving a query hit message which contains the file and its size. The route taken back is the reverse of what came from pre-existing TCP connection. If a query hit is given by more than 1 peer, then A will select any 1 peer for processing, say it selects the machine B. Then a client TCP connection is formed between A and B and A sends an HTTP GET message to which B sends a response message. This is done outside of overlay network.

<u>Combination of Centralized and Decentralized Approach</u>

KaZaA is an approach for locating content. It borrows idea from centralized Napster and decentralized Gnutella. KaZaA is similar to Gnutella as it does not use a dedicated server for finding contents. At the same time it differs from Gnutella that the peers are not equal. Here some peers act as group leaders and others are ordinary peers. The group leaders are given greater responsibility than ordinary peers. About a few hundred peers are assigned to a group leader peer.

When a peer launches KaZaA, it connects to its group leader with a TCP connection. The peer then tells its group leader the files it has for sharing. A group leader maintains database of all its children containing their IP addresses, files identifiers etc. Here a group leader acts like a Napster. At the sane time it differs from Napster as the group leader is not a centralized server.

Where Big Circle is for group leaders, small for ordinary peers and edges are overlay Peers use keywords to find the file just like a search engine works. A peer sends keywords to its group leader. The group leader replies by giving a list of peers that have the keyword. It sends back the list of IP addresses, identifiers of file and descriptors of files containing the keyword. If the file is not found in the peers attached to the group leader, then the group leader forwards the query to other group leaders.

2.7 Network File System (NFS)

NFS is used in a client server platform where multiple clients are served via a few servers. The server has the data stored on its disks and the client sends a request to fetch that data. This distributed systems set up helps to achieve the following:

1) Easy Sharing od Data

2) Centralized Administration can be done

3) The security needs to be provided to the servers to secure their data

The network file system is said to be transparent. This means that if a client issues a system call such as read(), write(), open() or close(). Then the server processes the request and sends back the response. For the user working on the client side, he does not come to know whether the data was retrieved from its local disk or from the server's disk. For the client, the service is transparent and no special API is used. The client gives commands to service the system calls.

NFS uses either UDP or TCP for retrieving data from the server. NFS is neither a secure or a reliable protocol. NFS uses remote procedure calls (RPC) to route requests between client and servers. NFS is also a stateless protocol, which means no state information is kept during processing.

2.8 Simple Network Management Protocol

SNMP is used to monitor the network devices on a local area network (LAN) or a wide area network (WAN). Other functionalities include detecting network faults and configuring remote devices. The network devices are such as routers, servers, printers etc.

SNMP is an application layer protocol using client server paradigm. The components of SNMP include

    1) An SNMP Manager

    2) An SNMP agent

    3) A Management Information Base (MIB)

An SNMP manager is basically a client, which calls an SNMP agent which is a server and the MIB is the database used by the server to get information. The SNMP agents are put on network devices which inform the network management system of their status and configuration details. The MIB stores the status information and description of the network devices. SNMP can monitor services like DHCP in addition to taking care of the h/w devices.

The SNMP agent sends information to the network management system when a serious event like a trap takes place. A trap is said to occur if the network crosses a pre-defined threshold limit. The SNMP agent constantly monitors the status information of devices.

2.9 Remote Login -rlogin

A host in one part of the network connects to a host on a remote part over the TCP/IP networking protocol suite. The remote login can either be done by rlogin command or telnet command. These two (rlogin and telnet) are considered to be alternatives to each other and perform the same task.

The server of rlogin has a daemon running in the background known as rlogind. The server keeps listening at port no 153 for incoming requests from the client. The client side calls the rlogin command from his terminal and specifies the name of the server. The client makes a TCP connection to the server.

The server replies with the following:

    1) The login name of the user on the client machine

    2) The login name of the user that it wants to use on the server machine

    3) Control information such as terminal type

2.10 Cryptography

Cryptography is a technique where we hide the message and send over the network such that the person for whom the message is intended, is the only one who can read it.

This hiding of message can be done by the sender encrypting the message and the receiver decrypting the message. Encryption is a technique in which the user converts the plain text into cipher text and sends over the network the cipher text. The cipher text becomes jumbled on encryption and therefore is not in a user readable form. The receiver on the other hand receives the message and decrypts it, that is converts from the cipher text to plain text so that it becomes in a user readable form and therefore receives the message which was intended for him.

The encryption and decryption is carried out with the help of algorithms and keys so that the cipher text becomes impossible to break. To develop complex codes which hide the meaning of message, we require disciplines like mathematics, computer science and engineering.

<u>The Goals of Cryptography</u>

There are three main goals of cryptography:

    1) Data Confidentiality

    2) Data Integrity

    3) Data Authentication

Data Confidentiality means that the data when travels over the network is confidential or private. The meaning of message is hidden by encoding it. To encode we need a cryptographic key. The cryptographic key for sender and receiver may be same or it may be different for the sender and receiver.

Data Integrity means that the message after traveling over the network should be same as was transmitted. Which means no modification was done in transmitting. No extra character was added, removed or modified during transmission. A technique called Hashing is used for verification. A hash value is created on the message and sent along with the message known as message digest. On receiving at the receivers side the message digest is compared with the newly calculated value by applying the same algorithm on the message. If the values match, then there is no transmission error, if the values differ, that means the message has been changed.

Data Authentication means that the user can prove to the receiver, that he is the only one who is sending the message and no body else is impersonating him. That is the data is coming from the correct source which the receiver is expecting and no body in the middle has taken control over the network and is sending messages that are expected from the original source.

<u>Attacks</u>

Attacks in cryptography are done so that the malicious user can get hold of the keys with which encryption, decryption is done. Also he may try to decipher the cipher text passing over network. His main aim is to know the plain text so that he can understand the code.

There are two types of attacks:

    1) Passive Attack

    2) Active Attack

Passive attacks are done where there is no modification of the data, only eavesdropping or listening to the network is going on. Active attacks happen when the user gets to modify the data and data is tampered with.

The following types of attacks take place:

1) Brute Force Attack

This means try all possible solutions until you get the answer. Suppose we have a 10 bit key, then the possible combinations can be 210 possible values, means 1024 different values. So the malicious users tries all possible combinations of 10 bits which are 1024 to discover the key.

2) Man in the middle attack

This takes place in public key cryptosystems. Suppose A wants to send something to B and therefore requests B for his public key. An attacker C intercepts the message and sends A his own public key. The attacker C can then read whatever is sent from A to B. To allow the communication to take place, he re-encrypts the data after reading with his public key and sends to B. Also he sends his own public key as A's public key to B, so that B thinks that the data is coming from A.

3) Masquerade

This happens when one person is pretending to be another entity. This is an active attack in which different information can be sent by pretending to be someone else

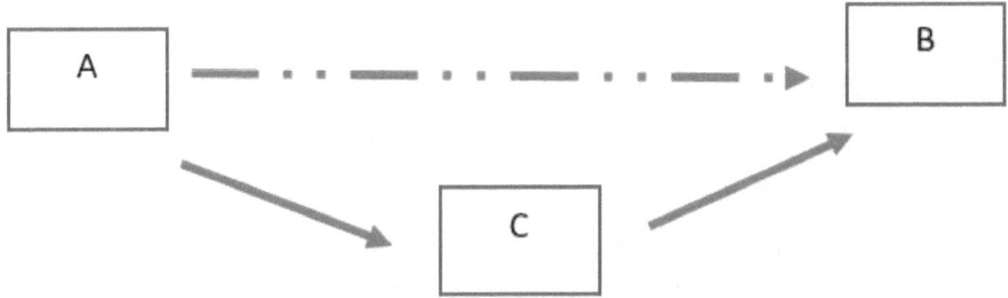

Here A wants to Send data to B. C is pretending to be A and is doing communication with B.

4) Non Repudiation

If A sends anything to B, then later on A cannot claim that he has not sent anything. On the other hand, if B receives something, then later on he can not deny that he has not received.

5) Replay

This takes place when suppose a malicious user say C captures data coming from say source A and intended for B. C in between captures data and sends at a later time, or send twice or thrice to B.

6) Denial of Service

This attack takes place when say A wants to send data to B and someone in between overloads the network by passing numerous packets on the network so that the system is disrupted and A cannot send message to B because the network is overloaded and A cannot provide the service to B.

7) Traffic Analysis

This is a type of passive attack, in which the malicious user is just monitoring the network and not doing any changes. This is used to help decipher the cipher text. In the analysis he is observing which letter of the alphabet is sent the most and which one is send the least. This can then be compared with English language. In English language the frequency of alphabet 'E' and 'T' is most, so the highest frequency alphabet over the network can be replaced by 'E' followed by 'T' and then slowly the message can be constructed until it starts to make sense.

<u>Encryption and Decryption</u>

Encryption means to convert a meaningful plain text into meaningless cipher text with the help of cryptographic keys.

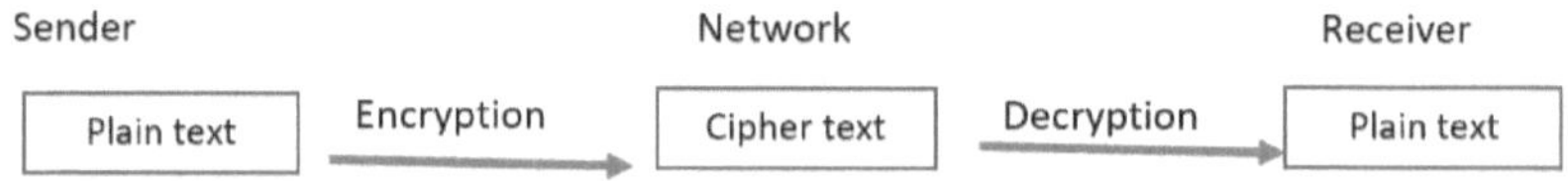

Encryption takes place at the sender's side and decryption takes place at receiver's side. A message can be encrypted with either with private key or public key. Similarly decryption can also be done with either public key or private key.

<u>Public and Private keys</u>

A private key is also known as a symmetric key or a secret key. A public key is also known as an asymmetric key. Private key is shared in a secret manner between the sender and the receiver and they both use this private key for encryption as well as for decryption.

A public key is used in a pair with a private key. The sender uses a public key to encrypt a message and the private pair key is used to decrypt the message. With the public key cryptography, a lot of users can use the same public key for encryption and only the one receiver who has the private key pair of public key can decrypt the message.

In public key cryptography two keys are used, one public and the other private. In private key cryptography only one private key is used. The public key can be used by anyone. For cryptographic algorithms such as RSA, DSA etc, the public key is used. The public key can be used in email systems to send messages in mail box. Public keys can be used where wide distribution of keys are required and it is practically not possible for every sender and receiver to share their unique private keys.

Private key Cryptography

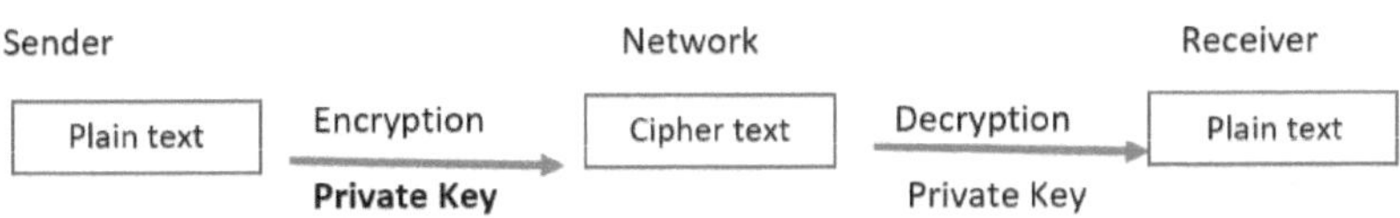

Public key Cryptography

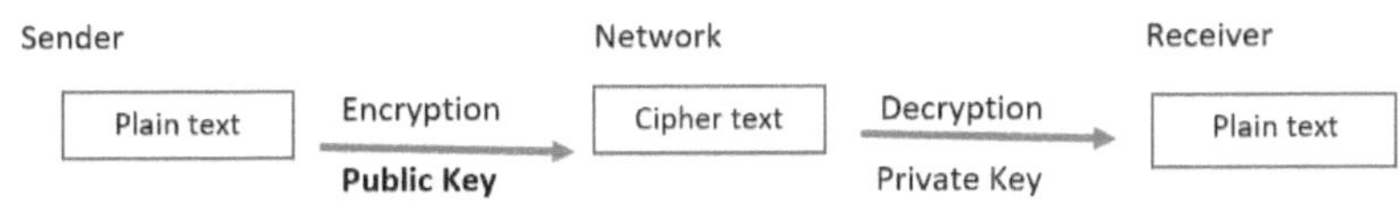

<u>Applications of Cryptography</u>

1) Encryption/Decryption in email

If a number of users are using the same mail, for example Gmail. Then the users use a common public key to encrypt the message and they send over the network to the Gmail server. The mails are intended for a particular user. This user can then decrypt the mail with his private key. The message of the mail traveling over the network is in a jumbled form and therefore no body can understand it.

2) Digital Signature

As the name suggests, it is a signature which is used to sign digital documents. Suppose a person signs a document digitally, so later on he cannot deny that he has not signed it (non repudiation). Also it provides authenticity, that means if someone has signed it then he is the only person who has signed it and nobody else can claim later on that they have signed it.

A digital signature uses public key private key pair again. Here the user who is signing uses a private key to sign the document and the recipients can be many, which can access the message by decrypting with the corresponding public key of the private key public key pair. How is this done? let us take a look. A hash function is used to create a message digest. This message digest is the digital signature. The message digest is then encrypted with the private key of sender A. The message digest is attached to the message and sent over the network to recipient B. B now decrypts the signature or the message digest with his public key and this results in the original message digest. To verify that this is indeed the message digest, B uses the same hash function used on the sender side to create the message digest again. If this message digest matches with the one sent by A, then the digital signature is verified. These digital signatures are used in high courts or supreme courts to verify identity of users who have sent it.

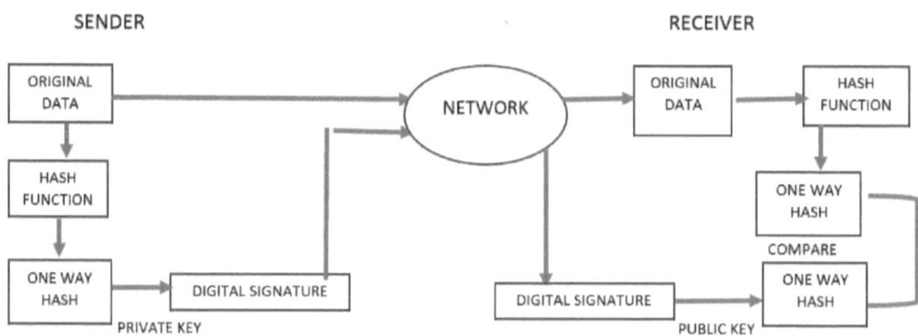

3) Whatsapp

In this a combination of asymmetric key cryptography and symmetric key cryptography takes place. The symmetric key ensures that the data is confidential and integral whereas the asymmetric key ensures that the data is authenticated and is non repudiated. Also elliptic curve Diffie Hellman algorithm is used to share secret key between the sender and the receiver without either parties sending keys to each other in a secret manner. This system is said to use end to end encryption. End to End encryption means that only the data is encrypted. All routing information, headers and trailers are not encrypted.

2.11 Firewalls

Before we end our chapter, we need to focus on yet another concept applied in network security and that is Firewalls. Firewall is a networking device who's role is to check the incoming and outgoing traffic on the network. This is installed to make sure that unauthorized sites are not visited on the network. This acts as a barrier between the intranet of the organization and the internet of the world.

A firewall checks the source and destination addresses of the packets, if they are directed towards unauthorized sites, they will be dropped and not forwarded to the machine. If the incoming traffic is intended for an authorized site, then it will allow the packet to enter.

2.12 Content Based Routing (CBR)

This is based on the concept that you can send packets to different destinations based on the content they are carrying. The content can have specific values on the basis of which you can segregate. Suppose that if we have a field called order_id, then if its value is 1, we can route to a FTP protocol, and if the value is 2, we can route it to an HTTP protocol. Generally theses kind of routing rules are established and therefore we can send to different machines.

2.13 SMTP Revisited

SMTP is an application layer protocol that runs over TCP at port no 25 of both the sender's and the receiver's machine. There are 2 distinct components of SMTP:

    1) The SMTP Server

    2) The SMTP Client

The SMTP client uses a transfer agent to send messages to the server counterpart. The server is incapable of storing messages in a queue and for that purpose it uses Post Office Protocol 3 (POP3) or Internet Message Access Protocol (IMAP) which have the responsibility of storing the messages in the mailbox and downloading them periodically from the server.

The SMTP server operates as a background process which is continuously listening at its port, when a client initiates a connection to the server, it creates a thread and lets the thread handle the request. After that it goes back to listen to more requests from the client.

SMTP is based on client server architecture. When the client wishes to send a mail, it will click on the send button. The client asks for a TCP connection with the server, the server forms a connection with the client at port no 25. The client uses a MTA (Mail Transfer Agent) to see that the sender and the recipient mail are from the same domain, in case the domains are different, then DNS (Domain Name System) is used to find the destination IP address of the server, The recipient then uses IMAP or POP3 to receive the mails.

Some common commands used in mail exchange are as follows:

HELO - The client identifies itself with the server

RCPT - This identifies the recipient's IP address

DATA - This is sent to signal that the data will be following now

QUIT - The client sends this to terminate the connection

RSET - This is sent to abort the transaction

2.14 Internet Message Access Protocol (IMAP)

This is a standard protocol used for retrieving the incoming emails. The mails are stored on the mail server and IMAP's functionality is to let the recipient view and manipulate them as if they are stored locally on the system. The emails are stored only at the mail server and at no other place. This helps the users access emails from any place and from any device. The emails are not tied to any computer and there does not arise any need for allocation of storage space.

IMAP follows the client server model. At one side is the IMAP client machine and at the other end is the IMAP server machine. IMAP protocol resides on the TCP/IP transport layer protocol which ensures a reliable connection between the IMAP client process and the IMAP server process. By default, the IMAP server listens to port no 143.

The functionalities of IMAP include:

1) Managing Multiple Mailboxes: By moving mails from one mail box to another, such as INBOX, SPAM, SENT etc.

2) Organizing Mails: Mails can be put into different folders which are created by the users.

3) Searching: The mails can be searched based on their contents.

4) Checking: The email headers can be checked before downloading any mail.

5) Synchronization: The mails are synchronized for all devices, which means if we delete a particular mail from one computer, then it will be reflected in the other computer also.

6) Downloading: Multiple files containing media are downloaded easily.

2.15 Post Office Protocol 3 (POP3)

The SMTP is used to send mails from the client to the mail server. The recipient computer then downloads the mails from the mail server and stores these messages on its local computer. Also it deletes all the messages on the mail server once that it has downloaded them all. Which leads to the face that no other machine is now in a position to download them again because the messages have been deleted from the mail server.

Advantages of POP3:

1) It requires less storage

2) It is easy to use and configure

3) It is supported by many applications

Disadvantages of POP3:

1) No real time synchronization of mails is possible

2) The mails cannot be downloaded again, once the first device has done that.

Differences between POP 3 and IMAP

1) POP3 downloads the message to the inbox of the local computer, whereas IMAP allows the messages to stay on the mail server after downloading.

2) POP3 runs on port no 110, whereas IMAP runs on port no 143

3) POP3 mail can be accessed by a single machine, whereas in IMAP mails can be accessed from multiple devices.

4) POP3 mails cannot be organized into different folders, whereas in IMAP various folders can be holding the mails.

5) All mails are downloaded once in POP3, whereas in IMAP message headers can be seen before downloading.

6) Contents of mails cannot be searched before downloading to local computer in POP3, whereas in IMAP contents of mails can be searched.

7) POP3 is fast compared to IMAP

8) Mails cannot be synchronized in POP3, whereas in IMAP, mails can be synchronized so that multiple devices can access them.

9) The user cannot create delete or rename a mail on the mail server in POP3, whereas in IMAP, the mails can be created, deleted or renamed on mail server.

2.16 Multipurpose Internet Mail Extension (MIME)

MIME is an extension of SMTP with an added functionality of sending non-ASCII data which includes audio, video and application programs.

The SMTP was unable to perform the following:

1) It sends messages only in NVT-7 bit ASCII format.

2) It does not support languages such as German, French, Chinese or Russian.

3) It not able to send audio and video.

MIME transforms non-ASCII data from the sender to NVT-7 bit ASCII data and delivers to the SMTP client machine. The SMTP server then connects the NVT-7 bit ASCII format to its original form. If audio or video has to be sent, then the sender would convert the audio and video to NVT-7 bit ASCII data.

The characteristics of MIME are:

1) Able to send multiple attachments within a single message.

2) The length of message is unlimited.

3) Audio and video attachments may be divided.

4) Able to send messages containing varying content.

5) Messages may have multi part attachments.

MIME works with SMTP and POP3. The MIME header is attached at the beginning of the original header and it provides additional information. The MIME header consists of the following:

1) MIME Version: Value 1.0

2) Content Type: Type of data present in the body of the message, can be audio, video or HTML

3) Content Type Encoding: Method Used for encoding the message, such as whether it has used 7 bit encoding or 8 bit encoding.

4) Content ID: This is a number used to uniquely identify the message.

5) Content Description: It defines whether the body of the message contains audio, video or images.

The Diagram below shows the working of MIME.

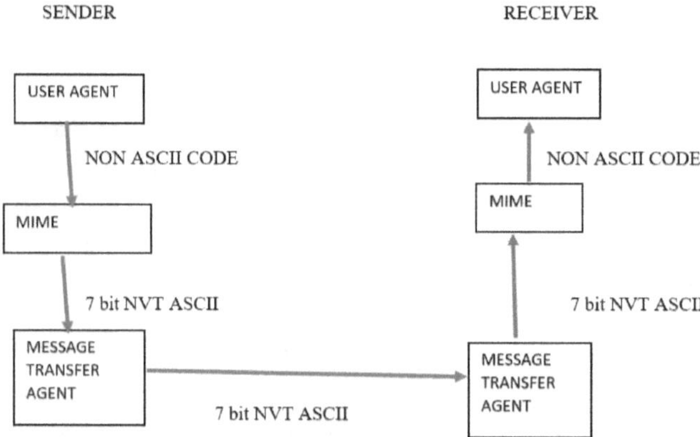

CHAPTER 3
THE TRANSPORT LAYER

3.1 Introduction

The transport layer provides the connection between two machines logically. There are 2 main types of transport layer protocols:

1) UDP – User Datagram Protocol

2) TCP – Transmission Control Protocol

UDP provides an unreliable connectionless service to the application running on top of it. Whereas TCP provides a reliable connection oriented service to the application running on top of it.

The transport layer packet is referred as a segment in case we are using TCP or referred as a datagram if we are using UDP. The network layer of TCP/IP stack also provides a logical connection between the hosts and is also referred as Internet Protocol layer. The IP layer service is called Best Effort Delivery because it does not guarantee that the packet will be transferred, but yes it does its best to do so. Therefore IP is also known as an unreliable service. For the internet layer, the connection is between machines based on the IP addresses, these machines run a number of processes on them. So in transport layer, the connection is between ports, each port identifies a process running on the machine.

UDP and TCP also provide Integrity Checking by putting error detection fields in their segment's header. TCP alone provides reliable data transfer by doing flow control with the help of sequence numbers, acknowledgement numbers and timers. TCP also ensures that the data reached is correct and in order. Also congestion control is provided by seeing that if a router is flooded with packets and is causing excessive traffic, then the rate at which the packets are sent is regulated.

The Transport layer does not have any knowledge of the destination host type, the underlying media over which it travels, the path it will take, the size of network or the congestion link.

A conversation exists when a source and destination connect and each such conversation is tracked separately. Also segments of manageable size are made because the underlying networks have a maximum transfer unit in which the segment has to fit. The transport layer attaches the header, identifies the application from the upper layer.

The host to host delivery is provided by the underlying internet layer and the process to process delivery is provided by the transport layer. At the receiver's side the transport layer receives segments from the underlying network layer. The transport layer has the responsibility of providing these packets to the appropriate application processes running on it. Remember socket pairs are made of hostname (IP address) and process (port number).

At the destination, the transport layer examines the fields to identify the socket so that the segment can be passed to the appropriate socket. The sender's socket is made the source IP address and the source port number. The receiver's socket is made of destination IP address and the destination port number.

Suppose there is a machine A and has UDP connection. It runs an application on port number 2222 and wishes to send data to port number 4444 on the destination machine B. The transport layer will create a segment putting the source port number field as 2222 and destination port number field as 4444. The segment is then passed to the underlying network layer.

When the segment arrives at the destination machine B, it examines the destination port number field which has a value 4444 and it delivers the segment to the socket identified by 4444.

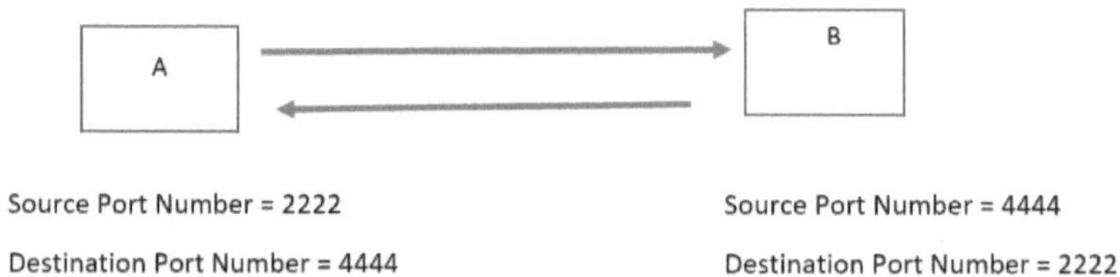

3.2 User Datagram Protocol (UDP)

UDP does not do any handshaking between the sender and the receiver and therefore it is connectionless. One application that uses UDP is DNS. If DNS wants to make a query, it constructs a DNS query and passes to the underlying UDP without handshaking. The host machine adds the header field (containing the source port number and destination port number) and passes the message to the underlying network layer. If a reply is not received by the DNS server, then it will either send to another DNS server or inform the source that a reply cannot be sent. UDP is not a reliable protocol compared to TCP which is reliable. UDP works on the principle of "best effort delivery", which means it tries its best to deliver the packet, but does not guarantee its delivery, because no acknowledgements and no retransmissions take place.

<u>Advantages of UDP</u>

1) UDP does quick work, as the data is passed to it, it constructs the header immediately and passes to the network layer. TCP does

congestion control and also it keeps on sending until delivered which adds more of congestion.

2) UDP does not cause any delay to establish connection.

3) No connection state is maintained, so no need to see send/receive buffers, congestion control parameters, acknowledgement numbers. The server in this case can support multiple active clients.

4) Header packet is small, so less overhead involved.

SNMP (Simple Network Management Protocol) is an application layer protocol which uses UDP because of the reason that network management works in a stressed way. The overhead of congestion controlled traffic makes it difficult to operate.

<u>Structure of UDP</u>

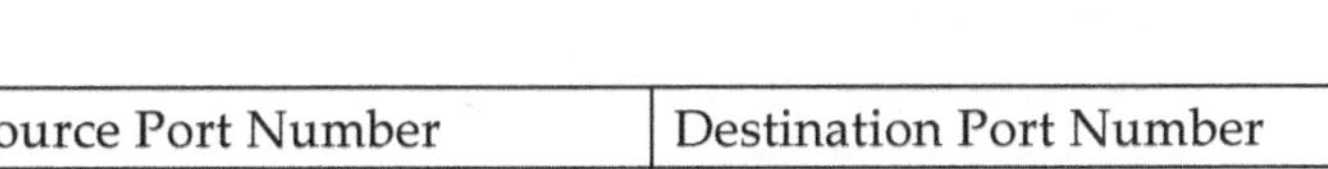

Source Port Number	Destination Port Number
Length	Checksum
Message (Body)	

The UDP header has 4 fields. 16 bit source port number, 16 bit destination port number, 16 bit length containing the length of the whole UDP segment(header and body), 16 bit checksum.

The UDP checksum is there to find out if the bits have altered during transmission. The sender side calculates the 1s complement of the sum of the whole segment stream divided into 16 bit words. And if any overflow occurs, it is wrapped around. The result is put into the checksum field of the UDP segment. The 1s complement is achieved by converting all 1s to 0s and all 0s to 1s. At the receivers end all 16 bit words are added including the checksum. If there was no error during transmission, then the sum will be equal to all 1s. If any error has occurred then the sum will not be all 1s but with at least one zero.

Let us take an example and see

Suppose there are 3 16 bit words that have to be transmitted:

Data 1   1001101001010110

Data 2   0000101110001110

Data 3   0000110111001100

Adding Data 1 and Data 2

      1001101001010110

      0000101110001110

      — — — — — — — — — — — — — — — —

1010010111100100 - intermediate

Adding intermediate and Data 3

    1010010111100100

    0000110111001100

————————————————————

    1011001110110000 - sum of all three data

Taking 1s complement of the sum to get checksum

0100110001001111 - checksum

At the receiver's end

Suppose no error occurred , then the sum of all three data would be that 1011001110110000

Adding the checksum to it

    1011001110110000

    0100110001001111

————————————————————

    1111111111111111

All 1s indicate no error.

3.3 Transmission Control Protocol (TCP)

TCP is a reliable connection oriented protocol. A connection is formed between the two hosts by a handshake mechanism which sends some preliminary segments to each other to indicate that now both of them are ready to transfer data. By reliable we mean that packets are sent, their acknowledgements are received. If there is problem in receiving acknowledgement , then retransmission takes place of that packet again. .

The TCP protocol maintains a connection when performing transfer. The underlying routers and switches are not aware of it, they see the datagrams coming independently. TCP provides a full-duplex service, which means both sender A and receiver B can receive/send data at the same time. TCP has a point-to-point connection which means there is a single sender and a single receiver.

TCP establishes connection with the help of sockets:

A socket is a {hostname, port number}. Hostname is the name of the machine that it wants to connect and port number identifies the process on the host machine. The client machine first sends a special TCP segment to the server. The server responds with a second special TCP segment and finally the client again sends the third special TCP segment to establish a connection over which the stream of data/ bytes will be sent.

This above process is known as the 3 way handshake. The client process passes a steam of data through its socket and sends data in the send buffer. The maximum amount of data that can be put in a segment constrained by the Maximum Segment Size (MSS). This segment size will be set accordingly to the size of the data link layer frame called the Maximum Transfer Unit (MTU).

3.3.1 Initiating a session

A 3 way handshake process is carried out to begin the session between two hosts in TCP.

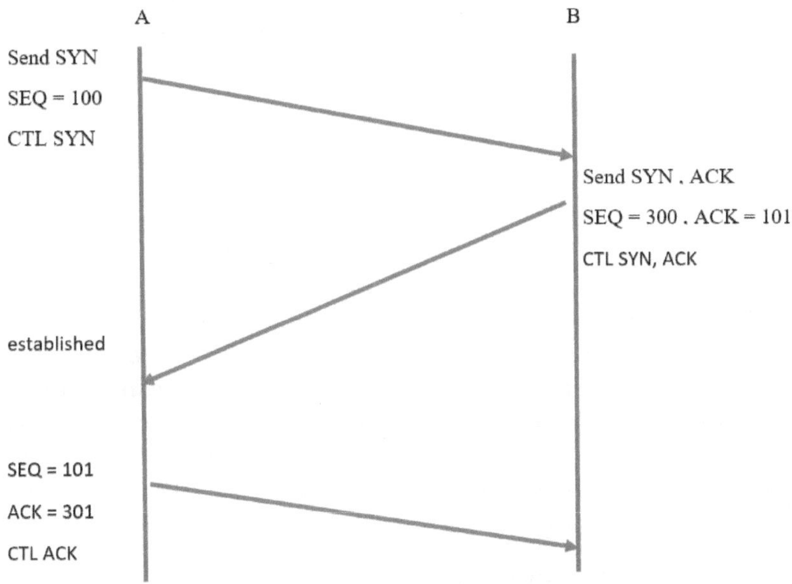

Step 1: Client side sends special segment SYN, it randomly chooses an initial sequence number and puts this number in the sequence number field of the TCP segment(100 in the above diagram).

Step 2: The sender extracts the TCP SYN segment from the datagram, allocates space for buffers and variables etc then sends a connection grant segment to TCP, normally called SYNACK segment. It chooses its own initial sequence number and puts the value in the sequence number field of the TCP segment(300 in the above diagram).

Step 3: Upon receiving the SYNACK segment, the client sends the server another segment to indicate that it has acknowledged the connection grant segment. It sets the SYN bit to 0, and adds 1 to the initial sequence number indicated by the client side(101 in the above diagram) and also adds a 1 to the initial sequence number chosen by the server side (301 in the above diagram)

3.3.2 Terminating a session

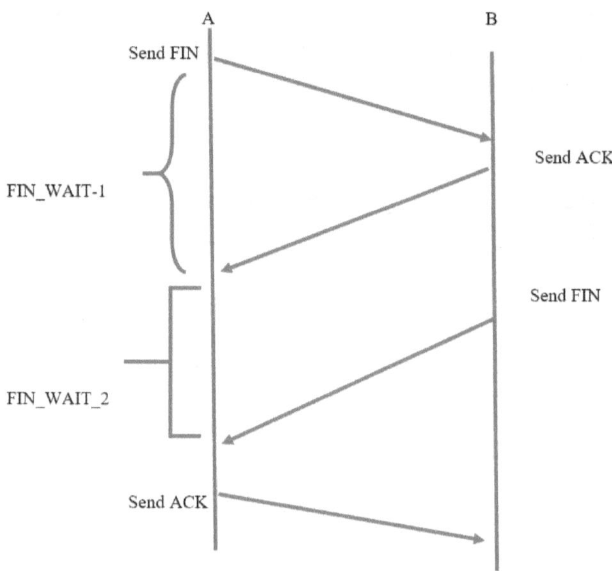

If say client A wants to close the connection, the TCP client send a TCP segment with FIN bit set to 1 to machine B. Then it waits for the server to acknowledge. This time limit is called FIN_WAIT_1. Once the acknowledgement arrives at the client side, the client starts waiting for another time unit called FIN_WAIT_2. In FIN_WAIT_2 the client is waiting to get a TCP segment carrying FIN bit set to 1 from the server or machine B. On receiving the above, the client sends a final acknowledgment to the server.

3.3.3 Round Trip Time (RTT)

RTT is measured as the time taken by a data packet to reach its destination plus the amount taken by its acknowledgement to reach the sender.

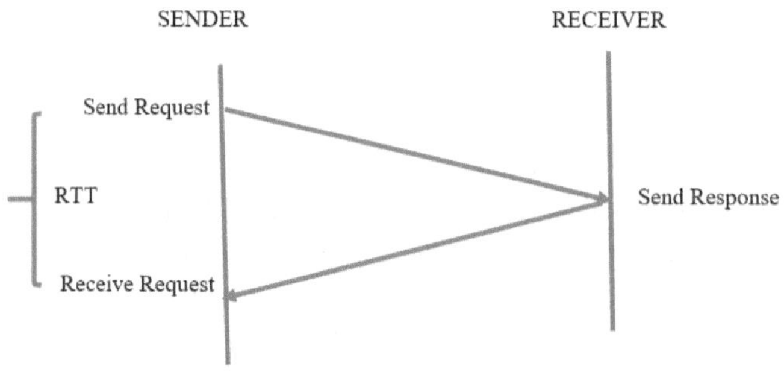

RTT is important because this tells how quickly is the network responding while browsing the internet. If the response is slow then the customer is dissatisfied. RTT is calculated as the sum of the following:

RTT = propagation delay + processing delay + queuing delay + encoding delay

Normally the value of processing delay, queueing delay and encoding delay is negligible, so mainly

RTT = propagation delay

Since we wait for the acknowledgement also so

RTT = 2 * propagation delay

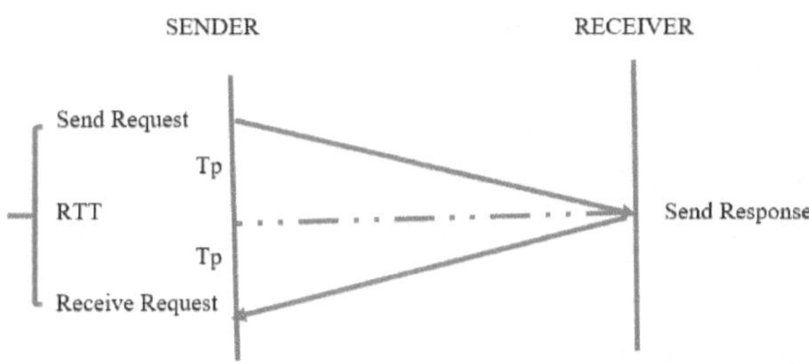

Here Tp is the propagation delay of 1 side.

So RTT = Tp + Tp

If there is more than 1 request to upload the page, suppose audio, video and images. Then if there are 10 such components, then

RTT = 10 * Tp.

for uploading the whole page.

RTT is measured by ping command. Suppose we do the following:

$ ping www.mail.yahoo.com

We will get output as:

reply from 124.6.7.3 10ms TTL 256

replay from 123.56.5.2 12ms TTL 256

....

So these values of 10ms and12ms are telling the RTT.

Another way to measure RTT is by traceroute command. The traceroute tells how data reaches from source to destination following all the routers through. It tells how much time has been taken at each hop. Suppose we do the following:

$ traceroute niu.net.edu

1 123.4.5.6 9ms

2 231.3.4.5 19ms

3 156.5.6.3 14ms

....

Here 1,2,3 refer to the hop number, the next field of IP address is the address of the routers through which it is moving. The next field time refers to the time taken to reach that router. The RTT will be the time taken by all the routers to deliver the packet to destination.

RTT is influenced by the following:

> 1) Physical distance between the source and the destination. If distance is large then more time taken

> 2) Response Time from the origin server. If the server is taking more time to response because of the bottleneck

> 3) Transmission medium. If optic fibres are used instead of co axial cables, then it will transfer faster.

> 4) Slow router. If there is congestion in the network, then it will be slow to move.

3.3.4 TCP Segment Structure

TCP segment is made up of the TCP header and the message or the body. The message body is filled by the data or message coming from the Application Layer. A TCP segment is formed by including the header and the body, this segment is then passed to the lower level network layer. The header of TCP is usually of 20 bytes long.

The TCP header includes Source Port Number, Destination Port Number which are 16 bits in length. It has a 32 bit sequence number field and a 32 bit acknowledgment number field, Also it contains a 16 bit checksum.

◄──────────── 32 bits ────────────►

Source Port Number				Destination Port Number			
Sequence Number							
Acknowledgement Number							
Header Length	Unused	URG	ACK	PSH	RST	SYN	FIN	Receive Window
Internet Checksum				Urgent Data Pointer			
Options							
Data							

A 4 bit header length field specifies the length of the TCP header, because the header length may vary if we have options field filled.

There are 6 flag fields:

1) ACK is acknowledgement bit and it is set to 1 to indicate that the acknowledgement for a segment has been successfully received.

2) RST , SYN and FIN are used for termination of connection. SYN is also used in forming a connection.

3) PSH is push which indicates that the receiver should give data to its upper layer immediately.

4) URG is used for indicating that this segment has urgent information and it is set by the sender.

Header Length

This field indicates the length of the TCP header. It is a 4 bit field which is also known as data offset.

Reserved Field

Reserved for future use.

Window Size

This is a 16 bit field which tells how many bytes can be accepted can be accepted at a single time.

Checksum

This field checks if there was any error in the segment header or data.

Urgent

This field indicates if the data in the current segment is urgent or not.

Sequence Number Field

TCP sends a stream of bytes over the network. Suppose A wants to send a stream of 6000 bytes to B. The bytes are numbered from 0 to 5999. Suppose the MSS is 1000 bytes. So 6 segments are constructed. The first segment gets assigned a sequence number of 0 and the second segment gets assigned a sequence number of 1000 and the third segment gets 2000 assigned and so on.

Acknowledgement Number

Acknowledgement Number indicates the next expected byte by B. Because segments may arrive out of order because the underlying network layer may take different routes if there is congestion etc.

Retransmission

Suppose B has received 300 bytes from source A. So B puts 301 as the acknowledgement number in the segment that it sends to A. Now suppose A sends B another bytes from 301 -600, and after that sends bytes 601-900. B had received first 300 bytes and after that it got bytes from 601-900, The bytes from 301-600 got delayed on the way. So B will send acknowledgment number as 301, because it sends the acknowledgment number as the first missing byte in the stream. In the above case the fragment 301-600 arrived out of order.

The following shows a normal working of sequence numbers and acknowledgement numbers.

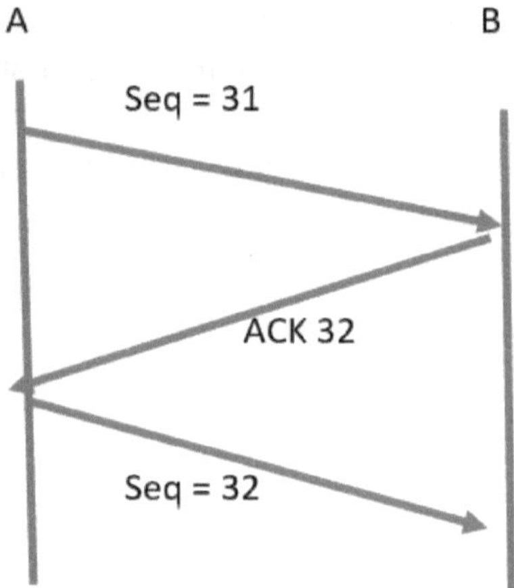

TCP provides reliable transfer on top of IP layer which is unreliable and best effort delivery. TCP uses sequence numbers and acknowledgement numbers to provide reliability. A major event that influences it is timeout. TCP waits for certain amount of time in which it expects to get acknowledgements. If the acknowledgement does not come within the time period, then TCP retransmits the packet.

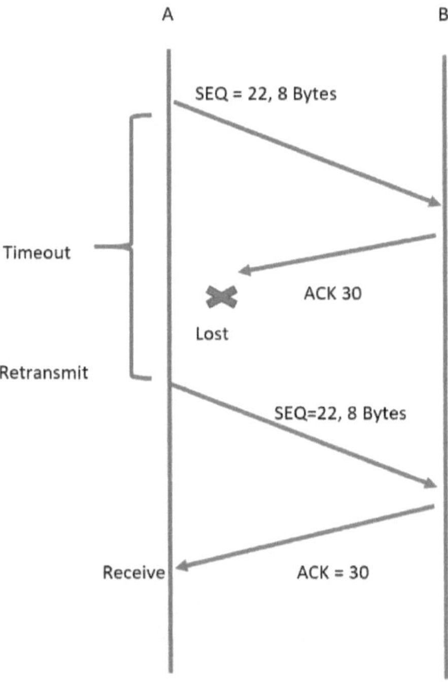

In the above diagram, it can easily be seen that A sends a fragment to B which is 8 bytes long, starting from sequence number 22. B is expecting the next byte of sequence number 30 from A , so it sends the acknowledgement number 30. The acknowledgement is lost on its way and A did not receive it. So A waits a certain amount of time to get the acknowledgement, when its timer expires, it retransmits the fragment. The retransmitted frame now gets acknowledged by B by B sending the Acknowledgement number 30 to A.

<u>The TCP Checksum</u>

The TCP checksum is created by the following fields:

    1) TCP Header

    2) TCP Body

    3) Pseudo IP Header

Pseudo IP header is not an IP header, rather it is part of IP header. The IP header is not used directly because the IP header changes continuously when the packets are sent over the network. Only that part of IP header is taken which does not change as the packet moves.

The Pseudo IP header contains:

    1) IP address of source

    2) IP address of destination

    3) TCP/UDP segment length

    4) Protocol used

    5) Fixed 8 bits

Pseudo IP header

Source IP (32 bits)		
Destination IP (32 bits)		
Fixed 8 bits	Protocol Field 8 bits	TCP segment length (16 bits)

After the calculation of checksum using IP pseudo header is done, then it is discarded. So the pseudo header is not transported across the network. The checksum is calculated using the usual method.

3.3.5 Flow Control

TCP hosts on both sides keep a receive buffer for connection. If the bytes arrive in order and are correct, then they may be placed in the receive buffer. The application process reads data from this buffer. It may read whenever it is convenient for him. Too much of data can be sent by the sender which may overflow the buffer. Therefore a flow control service is provided to remove the buffer overflowing problem.

Flow control is done by regulating the rate at which data is coming. The flow control is done by maintaining a variable called receive window. This gives the sender an indication of how much buffer space is available at the receiver. Since TCP is full duplex, therefore the senders at each side have their own receive window value.

For example, a typical host B will not wait until all 10000 bytes have been received before sending an acknowledgement. This means host A can adjust its send window as it receives acknowledgement from host B.

Consider the following figure:

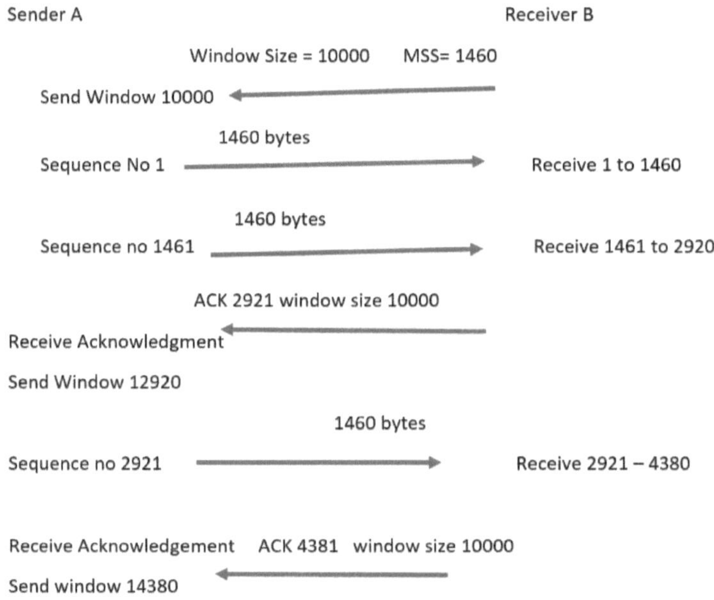

Here host A receives an acknowledgement number 2921, which is the next expected byte . Then the host A's send window increases by 2921 bytes and therefore becomes 12921. Host A can send upto 10000 more bytes to host B as long as it does not increase more than 12920.

A common Maximum Segment Size (MSS) is 1460 in an IPv4. A MSS is decided by subtracting the bytes of IP header and bytes of TCP header from the maximum transfer unit of 1500 bytes. In case of an Ethernet, the default MTU is 1500 bytes. Subtracting 20 bytes of IP header and 20 bytes of TCP header from 1500m bytes is 1460.

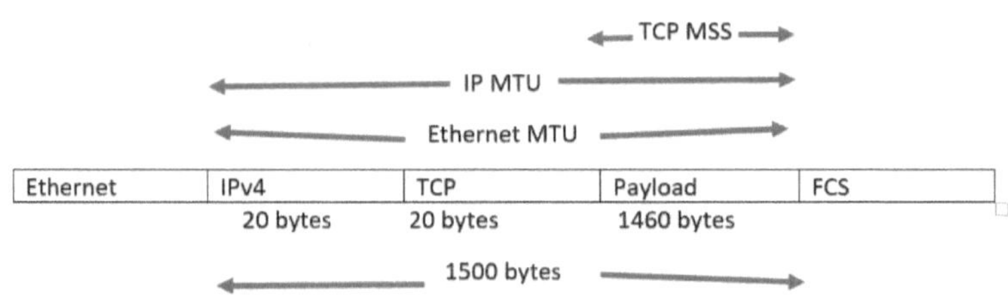

TCPs Sequence Number and Acknowledgement numbers behave as follows:

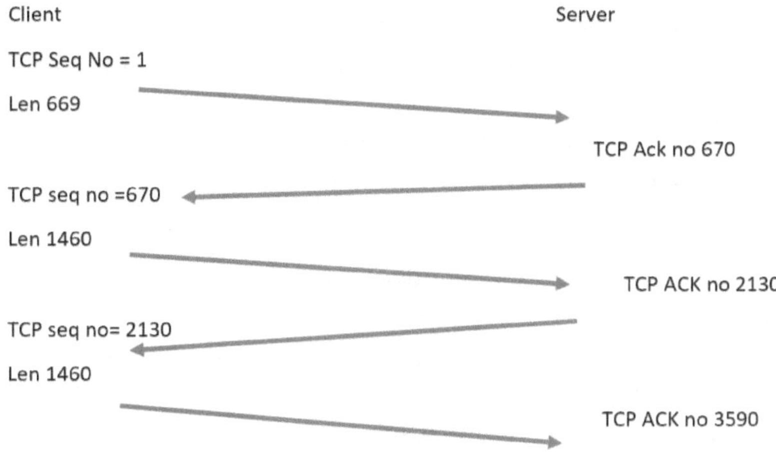

Continues until TCP closes.

3.3.6 Congestion Control

Congestion occurs due to the following reasons:

1) The input traffic is more than the output traffic. The queue is full and it starts to drop packets, the acknowledgement of dropped packets is not received, so retransmission begins and more and more packets line up for retransmission.

2) The routers are slow (they take more time to queue buffers and update routing tables.

3) The buffer of router is limited.

4) Slow links hinder in delivering packets, high speed links solve this problem.

The problem of congestion can be solved by two methods:

1) Prevent it from happening (Open Loop)

2) Take action after congestion has occurred. (Closed Loop)

Open Loop Congestion Control is solved by :

1) Retransmission Policy

In this packets are retransmitted if the packets have lost Retransmission timers are designed to optimize efficiency.

2) Window Policy

The Selective Reject policy is used over Go back N policy. The selective reject only retransmits the packets which are lost.

3) Acknowledgement Policy

Sending fewer acknowledgements reduce the load of traffic. The following approaches can be used to implement it:

     a) A receiver may send an acknowledgement only if it has a packet to be sent.

     b) An acknowledgment is sent only when timer expires.

     c) A receiver may send acknowledgment of N packets.

4) Discarding Policy

A router may discard less sensitive packets.

5) Admission Policy

A router may deny to establish a virtual circuit if there is a likelihood of congestion.

Closed Loop Congestion Control is solved by:

1) Backpressure

Suppose there are 3 nodes

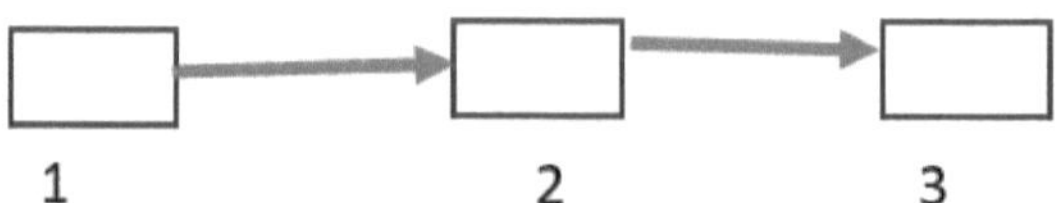

The traffic is moving from node 1 to node 2 to mode 3. Suppose node 3 is congested, then it will inform node 2 to slow down, node 2 in turn tells node 1 to slow down.

2) Choke Packet

The congested node sends a signal directly to the source to slow down. Here node 3 will inform node 1 to slow down.

3) Implicit Signalling

The source nodes sees that the arrival of acknowledgements is slow, so it guesses that there is congestion on the network so it slows down on its own.

4) Explicit Signalling

The congested node tells explicitly to the source or destination that the network is congested. This is different from choke packet, because in choke packet, a separate packet is used for informing. In explicit method the signal is used in the packets that are carrying the data. The signals can be sent in both directions, forward or backward.

In backward signalling, the bit is set in the packet moving opposite to the direction of data, or the source is informed to slow down.

In forward signalling, the bit is set in the packet moving in the direction of congestion. The destination is informed about the congestion.

If there is congestion in the network, then the sender slows down the rate at which traffic is sent into the network. If the sender sees that there is little congestion between itself and the receiver, then it increases the send rate. This is achieved with the help of a congestion window kept at both sides of the TCP connection. This restricts the rate at which segments will be sent into the network.

Let us see how a sender finds out that there is a congestion in the network. There is a "loss event" at the TCP sender side which occurs if

1) the timeout has occurred or

2) 3 duplicate ACK have been sent from the receiver

In case of excessive congestion, the router buffers experience path overflow which leads to the segments being dropped. This also results in loss event and gives sender an indication of congestion.

If we consider the case that there is no congestion in the network, then the previously unacknowledged segments will be received by TCP sender. Then the sender can increase the transmission rate by increasing its congestion window size at a slow rate.

Let us see an algorithm for congestion control called TCP congestion control algorithm.

<u>TCP Congestion Control Algorithm</u>

This algorithm has 3 parts:

1) Additive Increase, Multiplicative Decrease

2) Slow Start

3) Reaction to Timeout

<u>Additive Increase, Multiplicative Decrease</u>

The sender reduces its sending rate by decreasing its congestion window size. When a loss event occurs, other TCP connections passing through with the same rate also experience loss events. And in that case, they also start decreasing their own values of congestion window.

Now the question is how much size should be reduced in the congestion window, If the size of congestion window is 40Kbytes, it will reduce it by half making it 20Kbytes, and if more reduction is required, it will reduce by 10Kbyes. The congestion window size is not dropped below 1MSS(Maximum Segment Size).

Now let us see how should we increase congestion window size in the case that there is no congestion. TCP increases its congestion window size slowly. It increases CongWin a little (1MSS) as soon as it receives an acknowledgement.

<u>Slow Start</u>

When a TCP connection is established, the value of congestion window is initialized to 1MSS. During the initial phase, a slow start is done which means that the rate of sending is started slowly, but increases exponentially later.

Suppose at first the CongWin is 1MSS. An acknowledgement arrives at the sender side, CongWin is increased to 2MSS, After a while 2 acknowledgements arrive at the sender. The sender then increases the CongWin to each of the acknowledged segments, so it increases size by 4MSS. This is done until the time a loss event occurs.

<u>Reaction to Timeout</u>

If a loss event happens because of timeout, then TCP behaves differently from the case that a loss event happened because of 3 duplicate ACKs.

In case of 3 duplicate ACKs, TCP behaves by cutting the congestion window to half and then increasing linearly.

But if a timeout event happens then TCP enters a slow start phase, that is it sets CongWin size to 1MSS and then grows exponentially.

The above phase is done by maintain a variable known as Threshold. Threshold is defined as the window size at which the slow start ends and the congestion avoidance begins. Initially threshold is set to a large value of say 65000 Bytes. So initially there is no change. If a loss event occurs, then the threshold value is set to half of the current value of CongWin. For example if CongWin is 20Kbytes just before the loss event, it will be reduced to 10Kbytes and will keep that value until the next loss event occurs.

Traffic Shaping

Traffic Shaping means a method in which it is set how much traffic is to be sent in the network and at what rate. Traffic shaping helps to regulate the rate of data transmission and reduces congestion.

There are two types of traffic shaping algorithms:

1) Leaky Bucket

2) Token Bucket

<u>Leaky Bucket Algorithm</u>

In this we assume that there is a bucket which has a hole at the bottom. We pour water at random intervals in the bucket but the rate at which the water comes out from the hole is fixed. Also when the bucket is full we will not pour any water into it.

The input rate varies but output rate is fixed. This can be compared to the traffic in the network as if there is bursty traffic in the network, The bursty chunks are stored in the bucket and sent out at a constant rate.

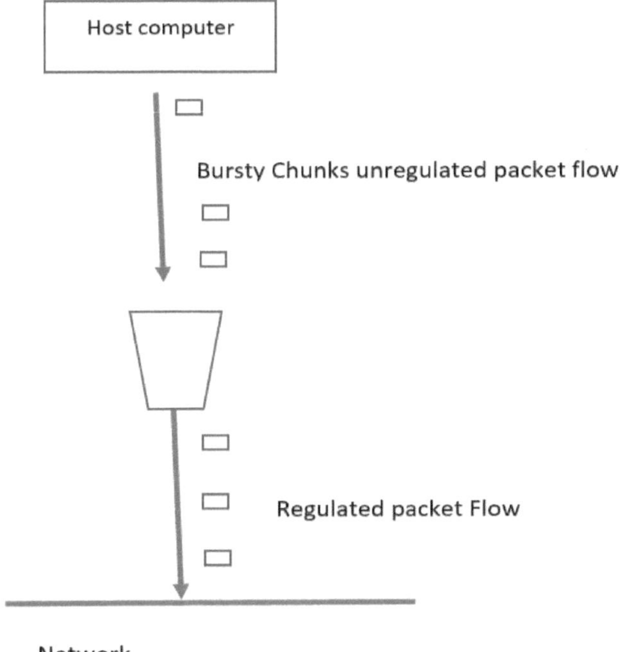

The host sends a burst of data at a rate of say 12 Mbps for 2 seconds. A total of 24 Mbps are sent. Then suppose the host is silent for 7 seconds. After that it again sends 4Mbps for 3 seconds. A total of 12Mbps are sent. In total 36Mbps are sent in 12 seconds. A leaky bucket smoothes out the traffic by sending constant rate of 2mbps during the 12 seconds.

A leaky bucket can be implemented using a FIFO queue. A FIFO queue holds the packets and a process removes a fixed number of packets from the queue at each tick of the clock.

The disadvantage with the leaky bucket algorithm is that it forces the data to come out at a fixed rate no matter what the amount of traffic is in the network. To deal with more traffic we take a different approach known as token bucket algorithm

<u>Token Bucket Algorithm</u>

The bucket has a maximum capacity of say f. At regular intervals, token are put into the bucket. If any packet is ready to be sent, it is removed from the bucket and sent into the network. If no token is there in the bucket, then packet cannot be sent.

BEFORE

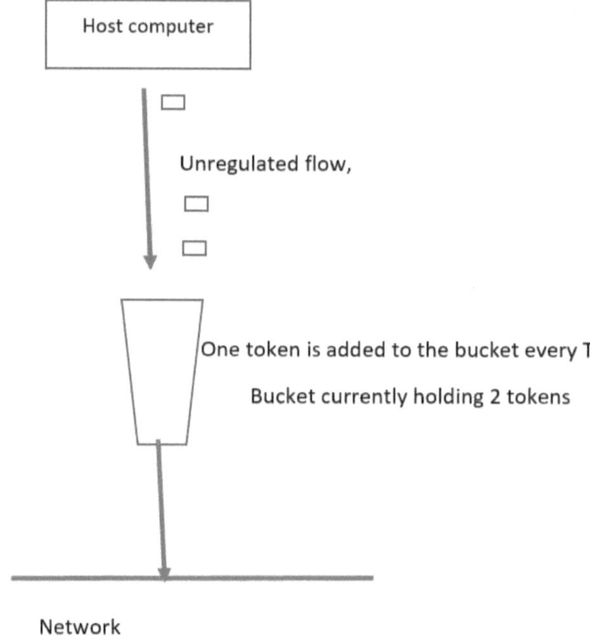
Host computer
Unregulated flow,
One token is added to the bucket every T
Bucket currently holding 2 tokens
Network

AFTER

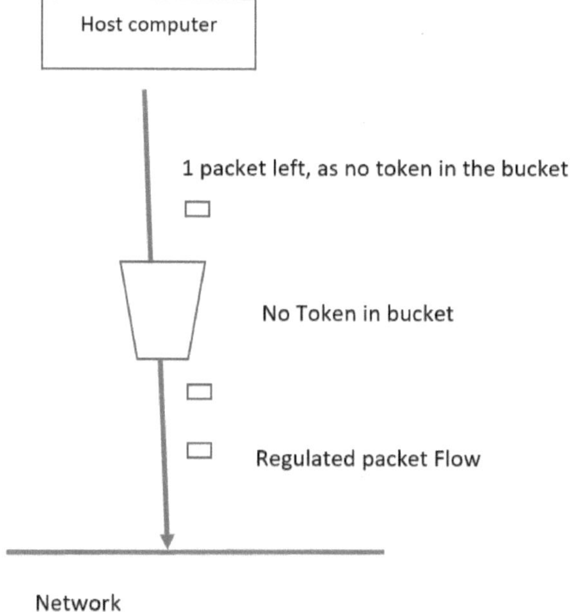
Host computer
1 packet left, as no token in the bucket
No Token in bucket
Regulated packet Flow
Network

In the above figure BEFORE, the bucket is holding 2 tokens, and 3 packets are waiting to be sent out of the interface.

In the figure AFTER, 2 packets have been sent out by consuming 2 tokens and 1 packet is still left.

Token bucket is less restrictive than leaky bucket, it allows more traffic to flow. Tokens available at a given instance of time in the bucket determine how busy the traffic is at that time.

Token bucket can be implemented by taking a variable counter to count the number of tokens in the bucket. Every t seconds a counter is incremented and is decremented when ever the packet is sent out. When the counter reaches zero, no further packet is sent out.

3.4 Stream Control Transmission Protocol (SCTP)

SCTP is a connection oriented network protocol in which multiple streams of data can be transmitted simultaneously. The data is reliable and in sequence which means all packets arrive intact and are in sequence also.

SCTP uses the functionalities of both UDP and TCP. It is similar to UDP as it provides message oriented data transfer. Also complete concurrent transmission of several streams of data called messages are transmitted between end points.

SCTP has a concept of multihoming which means it has multiple interfaces. These interfaces have alternate IP addresses, if suppose primary interface is unreachable or fails for any reason, then data can be sent to alternate   IP address.

Another concept of multistreaming is possessed by SCTP. In TCP we see that data in a single stream is transmitted known as a byte stream. And delivery is delayed if there is loss of data or out of sequence delivery. In SCTP data is delivered in multiple independent streams, if there is loss of data in one stream , the other streams continue and the entire transmission is not delayed.

With multistreaming, the client can open additional connections with the server so that the burden of servers is reduced. This is also helpful in multiple means of communication, like voice, video, shared applications etc.

SCTP supports full-duplex communication. Like TCP, it also provides flow control, congestion control and fault tolerance. Unlike TCP, it is message oriented than byte oriented.

The security in SCTP is better than TCP by the fact that during association setup, the identity of client is verified which later minimizes the possibility of man in the middle attack and denial of service. Also it is strong enough to deal with network flooding and masquerade attacks.

SCTP is reliable as it uses an acknowledgement mechanism to check the arrival of data.

The unit of data in SCTP is a data chunk . these data chunks are numbered. A stream identifier is also used to identify different streams uniquely.

3.5 Quality of Service (QoS)

Quality of service means that any technology which is able to manage the data traffic in order to reduce packet loss, latency and jitter. Latency means delay in network and jitter means change in the amount of latency.

QoS is able to control and manage network resources by setting priorities on specific data types on the network.

QoS is used by many organizations to meet the requirements of sensitive applications such as real time voice and video. Also it is used to prevent the quality and degradation of traffic which may have occurred due to packet loss, delay and jitter.

To measure QoS, the following parameters are used:

1) Packet Loss

Packet loss occurs if the network is congested and routers and switches start dropping the packets because their queues are flooded. In real time applications such as voice or video calls start experiencing jitter and gaps in speech.

2) Jitter

If the network is congested, packets start taking different routes and timings are shifted. In such a case degradation in quality of voice and video occurs which is known as jitter.

3) Latency

Latency is measured as the time it takes to travel from its source to destination. Latency in an ideal situation should be close to zero. When Voice over IP is used and latency occurs, then echo takes place and overlapping in sound occurs.

4) Bandwidth

Bandwidth is defined as the maximum amount of data that is transferred from one host to another in a given amount of time. QoS is able to optimize the bandwidth to improve network performance by giving priority to applications and giving more resources to applications.

5) Mean Option Score (MOS)

This parameter is used to rate the quality of transmission on a five point scale, with five indicating the highest priority.

QoS is important because it makes organized networks which are free from clogging. Also it avoids the complete shutdown of networks. QoS provides reliable service, which enhances the customer satisfaction.

3.6 Voice and Video over IP (VoIP)

In Voice over IP technology, an internet connection is used to transfer the voice and multimedia over the network as a digital signal rather than an analog signal which is used mainly in telephone lines. Here a broadband connection is used, and free calls are available wherever the internet connectivity is there. In this technology, voice signals are transmitted over the internet as voice packets, just like any other packet, be it sound or image that travels over the internet. Voice over IP can be used as video calls, conference calls and webinars with the devices such as mobile phones, computers and smartphones. Some services which the VoIP can provide are as follows:

1) Audio calls

2) Video Calls

3) Voicemail

4) Instant messaging

5) Team chats

6) Text messaging

7) Emails

Voice over IP has the capability to transform workplace in offices to work from home facility. The disadvantage of VoIP is that they are subjected to the limitations of bandwidth. Also another drawback is that the voice travels in packets, so it may be delayed and sounds can become jerky.

In Video over IP

In this technology audio and video content is transmitted in real time in digital format. Meetings, conferences and discussion groups can be formed by connecting devices without meeting face to face. A hub is used to connect devices having the data which need to be transferred. Once the data is collected, it is passed to the IP recorder. The internet protocol is used for the same, which in turn means that all devices are expected to have IP addresses. The data is saved on the cloud platform which is responsible for managing distribution of data in a secure, efficient and easy manner. The delays are almost negligible and therefore the transmission of data is of high quality.

CHAPTER 4
THE NETWORK LAYER

4.1 Introduction

The task of the network layer is to transfer the packets from source machine to destination machine. This is done by two methods:

1) Forwarding

2) Routing

Forwarding happens when a packet arrives at a router's input link, then the job of the router is to put it on an output link connected to that router.

Routing happens when the network layer decides a path that will be choose for transferring the packets from source to destination machine. The algorithms that decide the path are known as routing algorithms.

In other words we can put that forwarding does a local action, at which it just decides that the packet on its input link is to be put in one of its output link. Routing on the other hand does end to end network wide action of transferring from source machine to destination machine.

The router forwards packets with the help of a forwarding table. The router examines the header of the incoming packet to look up its destination IP address. It uses this value to find an entry in the forwarding table which gives the output link for the destination network id.

A simple example of a forwarding table.

Local Forwarding Table	
Header Value	**Output Link**
0111	3
0101	2
0100	2
1100	1

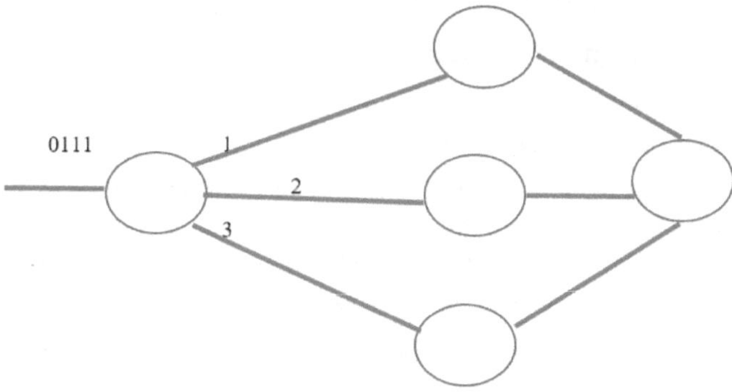

Every router has a forwarding table. The routing algorithm is used to put the values in the forwarding table. There are two modes in which the routing algorithms operate:

1) Centralized

2) De-centralized

In centralized way, the server has the routing algorithm running on it and other clients download the information from the server. In de-centralized way, every router has a piece of distributed routing algorithm running on it. In both the cases, a router receives routing protocol messages from which the entries in the forwarding table are put.

Network layer provides a service known as best effort delivery. In this, two considerations are made:

1) The timings between the packets are not guaranteed.

2) The order of delivery of packets is not guaranteed.

4.2 Virtual Circuit Network

In transport layer we had seen that UDP was connectionless and TCP was Connection Oriented. In network layer also we can have:

1) Connection Oriented Service

2) Connectionless Service.

In network layer also we have a handshake process for the connection oriented service and no handshake for connectionless service.

The host to host connectionless service in the network layer is known as Datagram Network and the host to host connection oriented service in network layer is known as Virtual Circuit Network.

The Examples of Virtual Circuit Networks are X.25, ATM, and frame relay.

A Virtual Circuit consists of the following:

   1) Path between the source and destination

   2) VC number

   3) Entries in the forwarding tables

A packet belonging to a Virtual Circuit carries a VC number in its header. The path is a series of links and routers. Each link in the path can choose an independent VC number than what it chose at other links. If we put the restriction that each path will have a common VC number on its links then the router will have a lot of burden.

In VC the connection state has to be maintained. Every time a new VC connection is formed, its entry has to be made in the forwarding tables. And every time a connection is closed, its entry from forwarding tables has to be removed.

<u>Connection Set Up in VC</u>

During the connection set up of VC, the following steps have to be taken;

   1) VC Setup – The transport layer contacts the network layer and gives the destination IP address and then waits for a connection to be formed. The network layer identifies a path between the source and the destination, which is the links and routers over which the packet will travel. Also a VC number is given to each link along the path and corresponding entries have to be made in each router's forwarding tables.

   2) Data Passing – Once the setup is done, all packets travel on this path only.

   3) VC Termination – If the sender wants to terminate the connection, then the corresponding entries from the forwarding tables of the routers are removed.

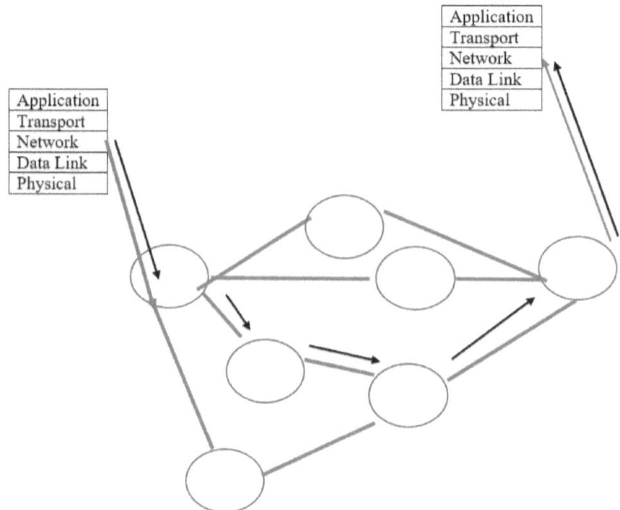

Consider the above figure, the routers are shown as ovals and the links to these routers with lines. A VC path is set up as shown by arrows.

Advantages of Virtual Circuit

    1) Packets are delivered in order

    2) The connection is more reliable

    3) The overhead of using full addresses is not there. VC numbers are sufficient.

    4) Less chance od data loss

Disadvantages of VC

    1) Switching System needs to be powerful

    2) It is costly

    3) Re establishment of network is difficult.

4.3 Datagram Network

No connection is required before sending packets into the network. Every time that a packet needs to travel, destination address of the packet is attached to the header and passed into the network. The packets in this travel from source to destination through a series of routers. Each router examines the destination IP address and determines where the packet should go next (i.e on which link interface) by looking up its forwarding table.

Suppose we have a forwarding table as follows:

IP ADDRESS	INTERFACE
200.6.8.0 to 200.6.8.63	0
200.6.8.64 to 200.6.8.127	1
200.6.8.128 to 200.6.8.191	2
200.6.8.192 to 200.6.8.255	3

Now if a packet comes with destination IP address as 200.6.8.161 then it goes to interface 2.

The datagrams are treated as independent units, no dedicated path needs to be set up as was the case in virtual circuits. The routing tables change dynamically and there fore two consecutive packets may take entirely different routes to travel.

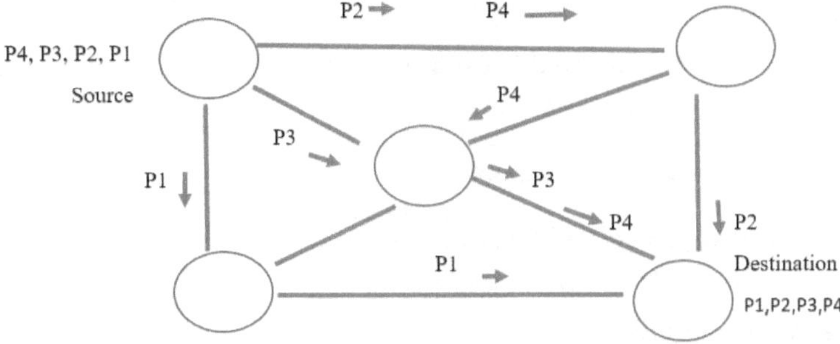

Here we can see that there are 4 consecutive packets P1, P2, P3, P4. They all take different routes to travel from source machine to destination machine.

4.4 Datagram Format

The datagram format means the fields that a datagram is made of.

◄————————————— 32 bits —————————————►

Version 4 bits	HLEN 4bits	Type of service 8 bits	Total length 16bits			
Identification 16 bits			0 1 bit	DF 1 bit	MF 1 bit	Fragment Offset 13 bits
TTL 8 bits		Protocol 8 bits	Header Checksum 16 bits			
Source IP address						
Destination IP address						
Options						
Data						

Let us see what each field means.

1) Version – This tells what is the version of IP datagram. It is either IPv4 or IPv6. We are discussing about IPv4 now. IPv6 will be discussed later.

2) Header length – This field is required because the length of the header of IP datagram is not fixed, it varies as we may include options or we may not include options.

3) Type of Service - This field is used to provide features related to service quality, such as for data streaming or Voice over IP (VoIP) calls.

4) Total length – the total length of IP datagram, i.e. header and data both. The minimum size that an IP datagram can have is 20 bytes and the maximum can be 65535 bytes. If the segment from the upper layer is too big, then it can be broken down into smaller fragments.

5) Identification- This field is used to assign unique ids to fragments of an IP datagram packet.

6) Flags: There are 3, 1 bit flags

Bit 0: this is reserved and has to be set to zero

Bit 1: DF or do not fragment

Bit 2: MF or more fragments.

7) Fragment Offset: This field is 13 bit long in length, and it is used to measure units of 8-byte blocks. These are used to specify the offset of a fragment from the beginning of the IP datagram. In the first fragment the offset is 0, this indicates that the fragment has started from this position in the datagram. In 8 byte 'blocks', if a packet containing 800 bytes of data is split into two equal fragments carrying 400 bytes of data, the fragment offset of the first fragment is 0, of the second fragment 50 (400/8).

8) Time to live: Time to live (or TTL in short) field is used to specify the maximum

time the datagram will remain in the network. The value that can be assigned to a datagram can be between 0 to 255. If a packet is delivered in time to its destination then there is no problem, but if the packet is not delivered in time then the maximum time it can live in the system is given by TTL. Every time that a datagram moves, its TTL is decremented by one. If a datagram is not delivered even after 255 moves, then it is discarded from the network.

9) Protocol: This field carries the value of the protocol used in upper transport layer of this datagram. For TCP value inserted is 6 and for UDP value inserted is 17

10) Header Checksum- This is calculated as follows. The IP header is divided into 16 bit word segments. The checksum field is stuffed with all 0s. Each segment is added to make the final sum. Then a 1's complement of the sum field is done and this is the checksum. Its value is put in the checksum field now and sent in the header. This is done by the source machine. The destination machine on receiving the packet verifies whether errors have occurred or not so it calculates the checksum again by the same algorithm which was used at the source machine. It then compares the value obtained to the checksum value that was received in the packets header.

11) Source IP address and Destination IP address- These are the 32 bit IP addresses of Source and Destination Machines.

12) Options – They allow an IP header to extend. Some datagrams might need them and other datagrams might not need them. The processing time of a datagram might also be delayed if options are included.

13) Data Payload – This field consists of the TCP or UDP segment passed from the upper transport layer. This segment contains the source port number and destination port number passed. The header of TCP is 20 bytes long, so if we remove the first 20 bytes

from this segment, the remaining data is the message passed from the application layer.

4.5 Data Fragmentation

The layer below the network layer is known as data link layer. This layer imposes a restriction to the amount of data that can be passed in a frame. Normally the size of the frame is 1500 bytes and it is also known as Maximum Transfer Unit or MTU. An Ethernet frame uses 1500 bytes, other link layer protocols may use a different size. If the size of the IP datagram is more than 1500 bytes, then it needs to be broken down into smaller pieces. The smaller pieces are known as fragments. These fragments are reassembled at the destination machine, no intermediate router has the responsibility of reordering them. To do reassembly, the destination machine needs the values put in the identification number, flag and fragmentation offset field of the IP header.

When a datagram is created, its source IP address, destination IP address and the identification number are put in its header fields. When ever a datagram fragments the source IP address, destination IP address and same identification number are put in its header. The destination comes to know that these are the pieces of the same datagram by having the same value in the identification number of each fragment.

Now the fragments may arrive out of order. If we want to know that there are more fragments coming, then the MF(More Fragment) bit of the header field will be set to 1. If it is the last fragment of the datagram then the MF(More Fragment) bit will be set to 0.

The fragmentation offset field is used to put the fragments in order. Let us see how we use this field. Suppose we have a datagram which is 6000 bytes long. So taking 20 bytes for the header, we have 5980 bytes to transfer. The size of MTU is 1500 bytes. So we will have to make 5 fragments as follows:

Fragment Number	No of bytes sent	Identification number	Fragmentation offset	More Fragment bit
1	1480	222	0	1
2	1480	222	1480/8 = 185	1
3	1480	222	2960/8=370	1
4	1480	222	4440/8=555	1
5	60	222	5920/8=740	0

4.6 Addressing in IPv4

Hosts have IP addresses and with that IP address they are connected to the network. Hosts have an interface between itself and the physical link. A router is connected to lot of interfaces, since its job is to take packet from one interface and pass to another interface. Each host and each interface of the router need to have an IP address associated with it.

An IP address is 32 bits long. So with 32 bits we can have 232 different IP addresses. The IP address is written in decimal notation or binary notation. For example, an IP address which is 4 octets (4 x 8 = 32) can be written as

198.6.81.3 and its binary equivalent as

11000110.00000110.01010001.00000011

Let us understand the IP addresses with routers and its interfaces. Consider the diagram below:

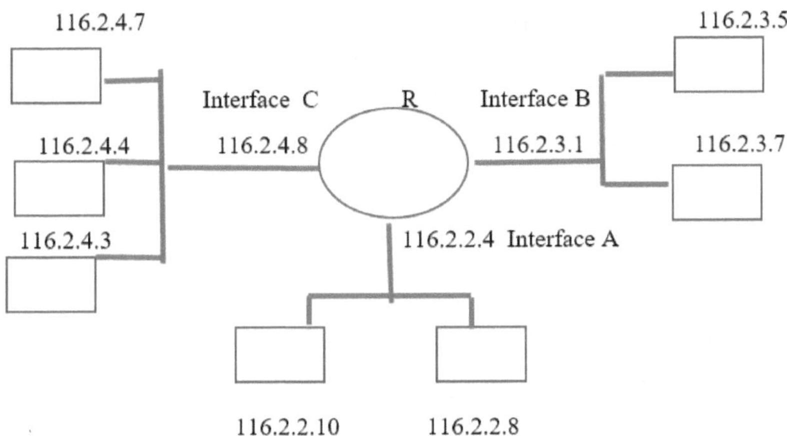

The router R has three interfaces which have IP addresses as 116.2.4.8, 116.2.3.1 and 116.2.2.4. Each interface has host machines connected to it. We can see that the first 24 bits of the individual interface is same as the first 24 bits of the machines connected to them. Eg 116.2.2.4 with 116.2.2.10. If a packet comes to the router R with destination IP address 116.2.3.x, (where x denotes any valid number) then it will be passes to interface B. If a packet with destination address 116.2.2.x comes, then it is passed to interface A.

Each IP address is made of network id and host id. With Classless Inter Domain Routing (CIDR notation), we put the number of bits representing the network id from left hand side with a slash (/) after the IP address. Eg 116.2.0.0/16. This means first 16 bits from left hand side are for network ids and rest 16 are for host ids. So we can have 2^{16} different network ids and 2^{16} different host ids. This technique is known as subnetting. If we have 24 bits from the left hand side representing the network id , then we can have the following subnets as

116.2.2.0/24 , 116.2.3.0/24 and 116.2.4.0/24. So we can have 2^{24} different network ids, each of which can have 2^8 different host ids. This notation is known as subnet mask. A subnet mask tells us which bits are reserved for network ids and which bits are reserved for host ids.

The above diagram can be seen as

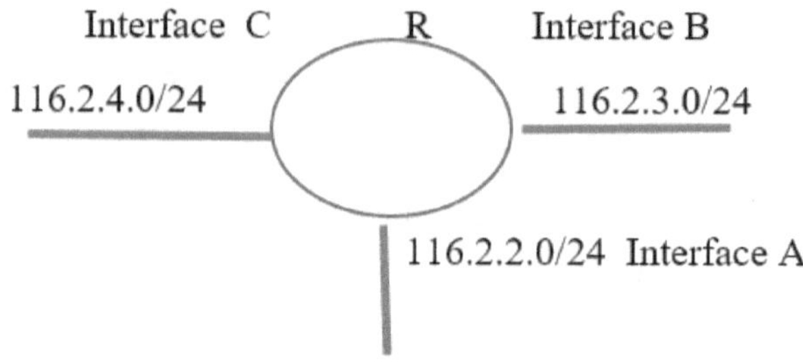

In the Classless Inter Domain Routing (CIDR), if a subnet mask was given as 226.4.3.0/24 , this meant the first 24 bits are for network id and the rest 8 for host id.

Before the invention of (CIDR), classful addressing was used. In this type of addressing there were 3 classes. Class A, Class B and Class C types of networks.

Class A

0	Network Id	Host Id

0 1 8 32

Class B

1	0	Network Id	Host Id

0 1 2 16 32

Class C

1	1	0	Network Id	Host Id

0 1 2 3 24 2

Class D

1	1	1	0	Multicast (28 bits)

0 1 2 3 4 32

Class E

1	1	1	1	Experimental Purposes(5-32 bits)

0 1 2 3 4 32

In class A type of addressing, the first leftmost bit is reserved as 0. The next 7 bits are for network ids and the rest 24 bits are for host ids. So the maximum number of networks can be

$2^7 - 2 = 126$ (the 2 are subtracted for all 0s network address and all 1s for broadcast address) and

$2^{24} - 2 = 16777214$ host ids (the 2 subtracted for the same reason given above)

The subnet mask for class A was given as

255.0.0.0 or 11111111.00000000.00000000.00000000

Where all 1s represent the network id bits and all 0s for host id bits.

In class B type of addressing, the first two leftmost bits are reserved as 1 and 0. The rest of the 14 bits are for network ids and the rest of 16 bits for host ids. So the maximum number of networks can be

$2^{14} - 2 = 163842$ (the 2 subtracted for the same reason given above)

$2^{16} - 2 = 65534$ host ids (the 2 subtracted for the same reason given above)

The subnet mask for class B was given as

255.255.0.0 or 11111111.11111111.00000000.00000000

Where all 1s represent the network id bits and all 0s for host id bits.

In class C type of addressing, the first 3 bits are reserved as 1 1 0. The rest of the 21 bits are for network ids and the rest 8 bits for host ids. So the maximum number of networks can be

$2^{21} - 2 = 20971520$ (the 2 subtracted for the same reason given above)

$2^{8} - 2 = 254$ host ids (the 2 subtracted for the same reason given above)

The subnet mask for class C was given as

255.255.255.0 or 11111111.11111111.11111111.00000000

Where all 1s represent the network id bits and all 0s for host id bits.

In Class D type of addressing, the first 4 bits are reserved as 1110. We do not allocate hosts, only used for multicasting. Here a single host sends a stream of bits to multiple hosts at the same time. Examples are audio or video streaming such as IP cables in an internet service provider.

Here the range of addresses vary from 224.0.0.0 to 239.255.255.255. The first octet varies from 224 to 239 because

The first 4 bits of the octet are reserved 1110 , so next 4 bits can vary from 0000 to 1111

Or 1110 0000 (128+64+32+0+0+0+0+0) = 224

1110 1111 (128+64+32+0+8+4+2+1) = 239

In Multicast addressing, the group of IP devices (also called host groups) are used as destination machine and never source machines, because they are more in number and we can have multiple destinations and not multiple sources.

In class E type of addressing, the first 4 bits are reserved as 1111. Here also we do not allocate any hosts. These are used for experimental purposes. They are not used for general purpose. Its range of addresses varies from 240.0.0.0 to 255.255.255.255.

The first octet varies from 240 to 255 because

The first 4 bits are 1111, so the next 4 bits can vary from 0000 to 1111

Or 1111 0000 (128+64+32+16+0+0+0+0) = 240

1111 1111 ((128+64+32+16+8+4+2+1) = 255

The problem with classful addressing was that there was clear demarcation on the number of bits being marked for network ids and host ids which could be done at the boundaries of octets.

Suppose we give just enough bits to be reserved for my network, 2^{24} would be too large and 2^{16} would be too small. I want something in between, say I want 2^{19} network ids and the rest 2^{13} for the host ids in each network.

So with classless addressing, the boundaries between octets is broken. My subnet mask can be something like this

11111111.11111111.11100000.00000000

Or

255.255.224.0

An IP address on the network can be written as 192.168.86.42/19

In this, the network id comes in the first 3 octets, so leaving the first 2 octets as it is, since they are all ones. Taking the 3rd octet for number 86.

Converting 86 into binary is equal to 01010110.

Now the mask of 3rd octet is 11100000, which implies that 3 most significant bits are for network id and last 5 bits for host ids.

So our network id for 3rd octet becomes 01000000. (64 in decimal)

Putting all 4 octets together the network id is 192.168.64.0

The first usable address will be 192.168.64.1

The last usable address will be 192.168.95.254

The broadcast address will be 192.168.95.255

Please note the hosts ids in octet 3 and 4 vary from 01000000. 00000000 to

01011111.11111111

01011111 = 95

11111111= 255

An IP address may be given to a system by one of the following ways:

    1) Manual Configuration

    2) Dynamic Host Configuration Protocol

In DHCP, a host obtains an IP address automatically. This is also known as plug and play protocol. In Manual configuration a host is assigned an IP address by the network administrator and every time the host logs in it is given the same IP address.

In DHCP, the IP addresses allocated are temporary. Each time that a host logs in, it is given a different IP address. The IP addresses are chosen from a pool of available addresses. This is used in mobile computing mainly or in peer to peer communication. When a host moves from one location to another, it connects to different subnets and therefore gets a different IP address.

Just before we study the next topic, a few comments on unicast, multicast and broadcast addressing.

Unicast – packets are sent to a single host. Examples: Email, FTP

Multicast – packets are sent to only a selected number of multiple hosts. Examples: Video streaming, online gaming

Broadcast – packets are sent to all hosts on the network. Examples: DHCP Requests, ARP requests.

The following diagram will make it clear:

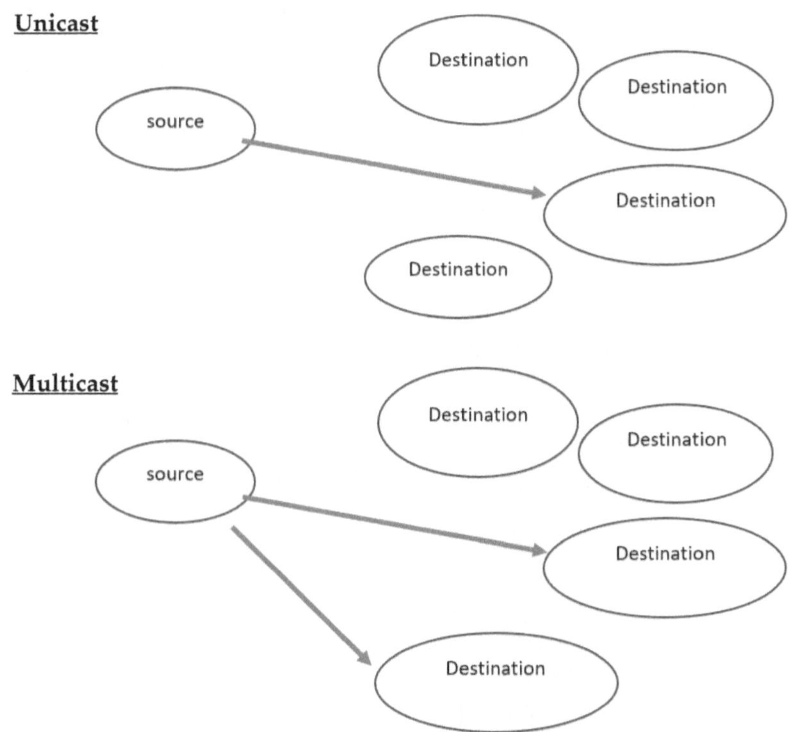

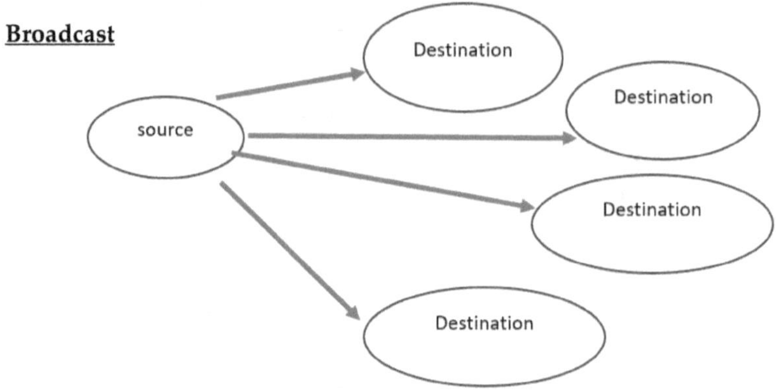

4.7 Network Address Translation (NAT)

There are two types of networks involved in this:

    1) Home Network

    2) Rest of the Internet

The home network has a router and its interfaces are like the ones described above. If from the home network we want to send to the world any message, then in the source address we will put the address of the NAT enabled router. So from home network any packet sent to the outside world will be a single address put in the NAT table. Similarly if anything from the outside world is coming for the home network, then its entry will also be found out with the help of the NAT table.

Let us suppose that the home network has an IP address 10.10.10.1 and the rest of the world has address 135.11.12.7. The NAT enabled router is hiding the details of the home network from the outside world. Any traffic from home to outside world goes to address 135.11.12.7 and any traffic from outside world to the home also goes to 135.11.12.7. The NAT enabled router has two sides, one is the home network LAN and the other is the outside world WAN.

NAT Translation Table	
WAN	LAN
135.11.12.7	10.10.10.1
5555	3333

The NAT translation table also uses port numbers along with IP addresses. Suppose a user on 10.10.10.1 wants to access a web page on the machine 122.119.4.6, so it will give an HTTP request with port number 80. The user then selects a random port number say 3333 and sends the datagram into the LAN. The NAT enabled router receives the datagram and puts another port number say 5555 instead of 3333 and the IP source address is put as 135.11.12.7 instead of 10.10.10.1. The NAT in the router also adds an entry in the NAT translation table. The HTTP on destination side is not aware of the changes done. It replies back to the NAT enabled router with the destination address of 135.11.12.7. NAT router on receiving the reply from HTTP puts back the original IP address 10.10.10.1, and forwards the packet into the LAN or home network.

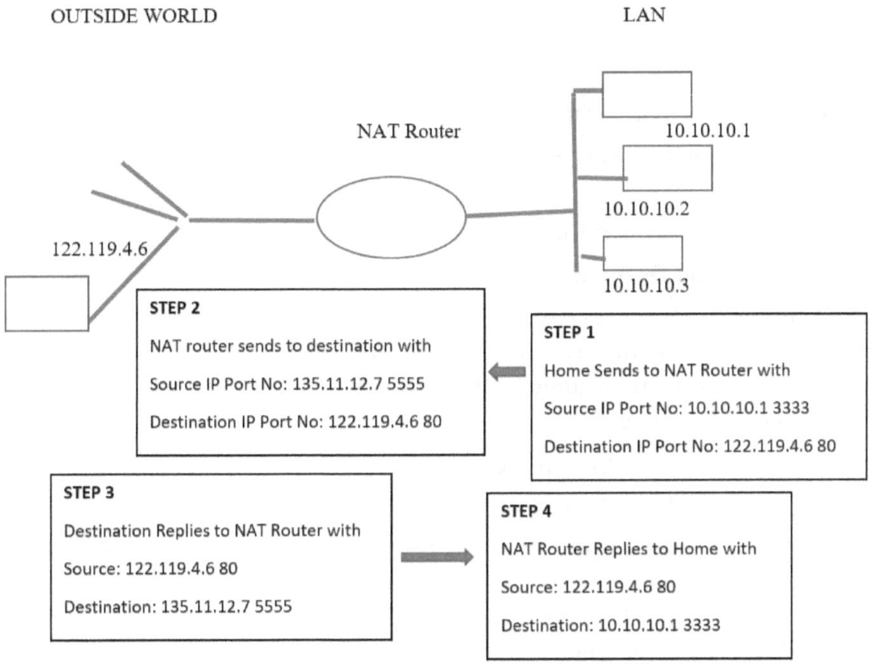

4.8 IPv6 Datagram

The 32 bit IP address were limited to having addresses upto 2^{32} . As more and more systems started to join the internet, the addresses were falling short for the new machines. Therefore the IPv6 protocol was developed to increase the number of IP addresses available. Here the IP addresses were 128 bits long. The IPv6 datagram is as follows:

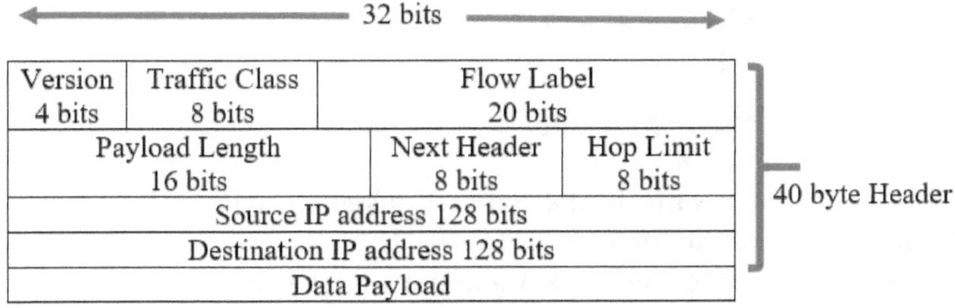

The following fields are defined in IPv6:

1) Version: This is the same as IPv4 field, it means the version of the IP datagram which is either 4 or 6.

2) Traffic class: This is the same as TOS field of IPv4.

3) Flow Label: This is a 20 bit field which is there to identify a flow in the datagram

4) Payload Length: The number of bytes is the datagram excluding the 40 byte header of IPv6.

5) Next Header: This is the same field as in IPv4 identifying the protocol.

6) Hop Limit: This is the same field as TTL of Pv4.

7) Source and Destination IP address: These are 128 bits IP addresses.

The fragmentation or reassembly are performed at the destination and source machines and not at the intermediary routers. The header checksum field is not there because already checksum is done in TCP layer and Data Link layer, so the designers removed from the IP layer.

There is no options field in IPv6, therefore the fixed 40 byte header is there and no extension of the header field is required.

Let us see the question that how do IPv4 and IPv6 versions operate with one another, as some machines on the internet still use IPv4 and the other machines use IPv6. Suppose there are 2 machines A and B as source and destination and both of them are using IPv6. Now intermediate routers in between use IPv4.

Here we use the technique called Tunnelling to make them work with each other.

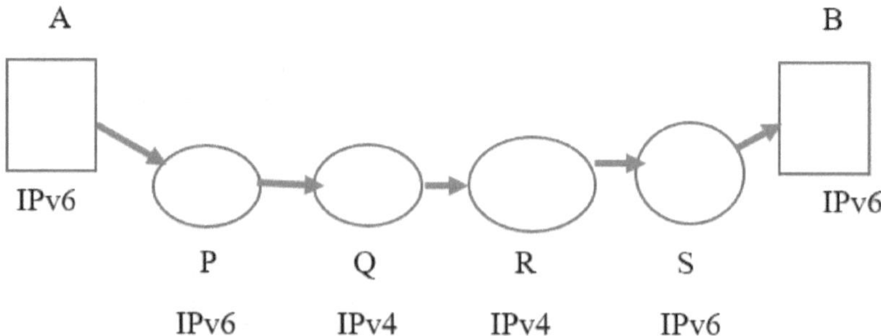

A wants to send data to B, the router P takes the whole IPv6 datagram from A and puts it into the payload field of IPv4. Then it sends to the first node in the tunnel which is Q router. The packet gets transferred to in between routers using IPv4 which are unaware of the fact that the IPv4 payload contains an IPv6 datagram inside it. The machine S receives an IPv4 datagram, extracts the IPv6 from it and passes to the destination B.

4.9 Routing Algorithms

Routing Algorithms reside inside the network routers, they exchange information among themselves and then put the information in the forwarding tables. The network layer is used to determine the path that the packets would take to go from sender to receiver. Routing does the job of determining the best path from sender to receiver through the interconnection of routers.

A host is always attached to its default router. Whenever the host sends a packet, it is transferred to the default router. Routing algorithms determine the best path. A best path is the one which has the least cost. A path is generally determined by a graph which contains the nodes and the edges. The nodes represent the routers at which forwarding decisions are made, and the edges determine the connections/ links between the nodes. The link has a value associated with it which determines the cost.

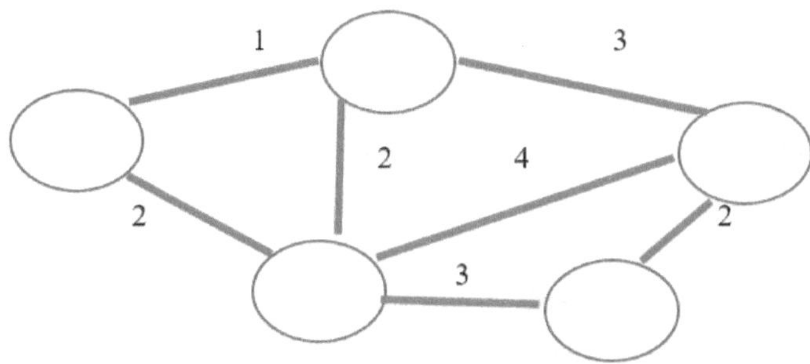

There are 2 types of routing algorithms:

    1) Global Routing Algorithm

    2) De-centralized Routing Algorithm

Another way to classify routing algorithms is whether they are static or dynamic. In static routing, the user needs to manually change the entries in the forwarding table. Whereas in dynamic routing, the forwarding table are changed according to the network traffic or change in the structure of network. By structure of network we mean the nodes are added or deleted.

Yet another way to classify routing algorithms is based on the load that routers carry. In this load-sensitive algorithm, the current level of congestion is monitored. If the traffic is high and if the node is facing congestion, then an alternate path is chosen to go around the route. Examples of load-sensitive algorithms are (RIP, OSPF, BGP).

<u>Global Routing Algorithm</u>

A global routing algorithm finds out the least-cost path between the source machine and the destination machine. It requires the whole global knowledge about the machines and the connections with each other as inputs to the algorithms and then actual calculations can be made. This algorithm is also known as Link State (LS) algorithm as it needs to know the cost of each link existing in the network.

<u>Decentralized Routing Algorithm</u>

In this algorithm, the path of least cost is not made earlier, it is calculated in repetitive distributed manner. The nodes do not have complete information of the costs to all other nodes, rather they start by knowing costs of their neighbouring nodes only. The nodes gradually acquire the information to reach the destinations. This type of algorithm uses the Distance Vector (DV) algorithm.

4.9.1 Link State Algorithm

In Link State, all links link costs are known and provided as inputs to the LS Algorithm. This takes place by all nodes broadcasting their link state packets to all other nodes in the network. This enables each node to have the complete view of the network. So each node is capable of running the LS Algorithm and calculating the same set of least-cost path as every other node.

The algorithm uses Dijkstra's Algorithm

Dijkstra's Algorithm measures the least cost path from one node (called the source node denoted as a) to all other nodes in the network. After m iterations, the least cost path will be known to m destination nodes and m paths will have m smallest costs.

The parameters used are as follows:

D(l) = cost of the least cost path from source node to the destination l.

P(l) = Previous node (neighbour of l) along the least cost path from the source to l.

N' = subset of nodes : l in the N' has the least cost path definitely known.

Link State Algorithm:

Initialization:

N' = {a}

For all nodes l

If l is a neighbour of a

Then D(l) = c(a, l)

Else

D(l) = ∞

Loop

Find k not in N' such that D(k) is minimum
Add k to N'
Update D(l) for each neighbour of l of k and not in N'

D(l) = min{ D(l), D(k) + c(k, l)}

/* new cost to l is either old cost to 1 or least cost path to k plus cost from k to l*/

Until N' = N

Consider the following figure:

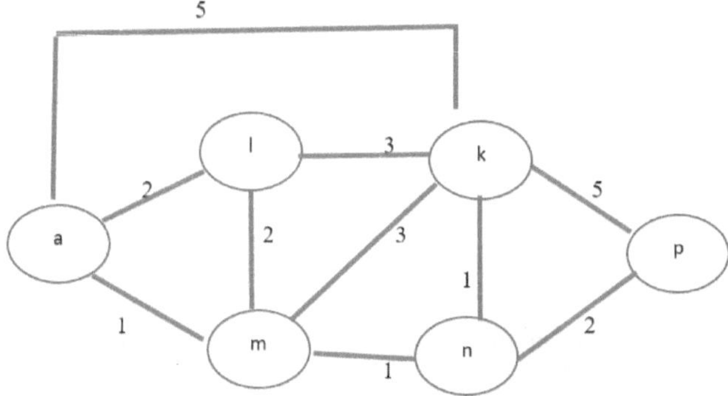

In the initialization step, the cost known to a and its directly attached neighbours l, m and k are 2 , 1 and 5 respectively. In the first iteration, the node m has cost of 1, so it is added to N'. The cost of path k which was 5 after initialization is now found to be 4 (from a to m to k). Hence this lower cost is selected and the path of k is set to go from m. k's predecessor along the shortest path from a is set to m. The cost of l is unchanged and set to 2.

After the link state algorithm is complete, for each predecessor, we have its own predecessor and the entire path can be combined from source to destination. This is the forwarding table of each node, for each destination, we have the next hop node as the least cost path from a to all destinations.

4.9.2 Distance Vector Algorithm

This algorithm does not use global information. It is distributed asynchronous and repetitive. It is distributed because of the fact that some information about the neighbouring nodes is calculated and given back to the nodes. It does so until no more information is available to be given to its neighbours. This algorithm is based on Bellman Ford's equation. The only information that a node has is the costs of the links attached to its neighbours and the information that it received from its neighbours. Each node waits to get an update from its neighbours, it calculates the new distance after getting the update and distributes the new distance vector to its neighbours. The neighbours then update their routing tables and this is how information is spread.

The Bellman Ford equation is as follows:

$$d_x (z) = \min_y \{c(x,y) + d_y (z)\}$$

Consider the same figure given above.

$$d_l(p) = 5$$
$$d_m(p) = 3$$
$$d_k(p) = 3$$
$$c(a,l) = 2$$
$$c(a, m) = 1$$
$$c(a, k) = 5$$
$$d_a(p) = \min \{ c(a,l) + d_l(p), c(a, m) + d_m(p), c(a, k) + d_k(p)\}$$
$$= \min \{ (2+5), (1+3), (5+3)\}$$
$$= 4$$

So the shortest distance from a to p is through m.

Each node's routing table includes it's own distance vector and the distance vector of all its neighbours. After initialization, each node sends its distance vector to its neighbours. After receiving updates, each node recomputes its distance vector, if new minimum is found then it updates its routing table and sends new updates to its neighbours.

For simplicity, consider 3 nodes, G , H and I.

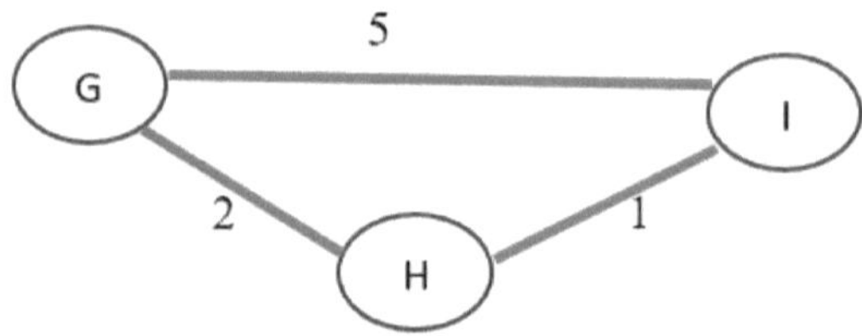

Initial Table of G:

	G	H	I
G	0	2	5
H	∞	∞	∞
I	∞	∞	∞

Initial Table of H:

	G	H	I
G	∞	∞	∞
H	2	0	1
I	∞	∞	∞

Initial Table of I:

	G	H	I
G	∞	∞	∞
H	∞	∞	∞
I	5	1	0

After 1st iteration, All nodes send their distance vectors to all neighbours. Note that the distances have been recomputed and minimum values placed (G to I = 3 instead of 5)

Iteration 1 Table of G:

	G	H	I
G	0	2	3
H	2	0	1
I	5	1	0

Iteration 1 Table of H:

	G	H	I
G	0	2	5
H	2	0	1
I	5	1	0

Iteration 1 Table of I:

	G	H	I
G	0	2	5
H	2	1	0
I	3	1	0

4.9.3 Hierarchical Routing

An Autonomous System (AS) has a group of routers that are all controlled by a single administrator, eg. the same ISP or all belonging to the network of an organization. The routers which are present in the same AS run the same routing algorithm such as (Link State or Distance Vector) and all routers have the same information about each other. The routing algorithm which is common to all routers of an AS is known as Intra Autonomous System Routing Protocol. With networks there would arise a need to connect different Autonomous Systems. Which will further introduce the responsibility of say at least one router to connect to the outside world. Outside world means AS other than its own AS. Such routers are called gateway routers.

Consider the following figure:

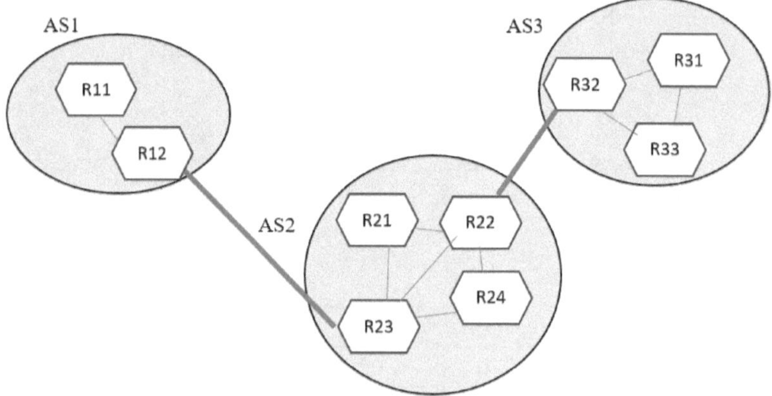

There are 2 routers in AS1 – R11, R12

There are 4 routers in AS2 – R21, R22, R23, R24

There are 3 routers in AS3 – R31, R32, R33

AS1 routers R11 and R12 run Intra Autonomous Routing Protocol within AS1. Their internal routers know how to send packets to each other using the optimal path.

In the above figure R12, R23, R22 and R32 are gateway routers that connect one AS to another AS.

Suppose now R31 wants to send a packet to AS2. It will either forward the packet directly to R32 or to R33, whichever is best according to its forwarding table. But ultimately it will be brought to R32, because that is the gateway router of AS3. This gateway router R32 will pass to the gateway router R22 in AS2.

Now look at AS2, it has 2 gateway routers, namely R22 and R23. Suppose a router in AS2 wants to send packets outside of AS2. Then this will be possible if we forward them to either R22 or R23. But the question is send it to which one? So we need to know which destinations will be reachable by AS1 and which destinations will be reachable by AS3. We will need to tell all routers of AS2 where to forward the packet if it is intended for AS1 and where to send if it is intended for AS3. The routers of AS2 will need to configure their forwarding tables accordingly. To handle this situation we will need another protocol known as Inter AS routing protocol. In the whole Internet, the same Inter AS routing protocol is used known as BGP (Border Gateway Protocol).

4.9.4 Routing Information Protocol (RIP)

RIP is a Distance Vector Protocol (DV) which works on the principle of hop count. How information is shared among routers in an Autonomous System (AS) is its major task. Each router of an RIP has a routing table of its own maintaining how to reach different destinations and how many hops will be required to reach them. Every router broadcasts its information every 30 seconds to its nearest neighbours. Nearest neighbour means routers connected to this router directly. The neighbours which have received this information pass it on to its own nearest neighbours and so on the information is passed.

Whenever a router receives an update for a shorter route to a destination, than its current longer route, it will update the routing table with the new path. If the update is for a longer path than its current path, then it will wait for a period called "hold down" to see that the route has stabilized and after that period, it will update the routing table.

If the destination address is of a router that is connected to the sending router, then the packet will be delivered directly with a cost of 1, or we say that the hop count is 1. RIP supports only 15 hops for a packet to reach its destination. If more than 15 hops are required, then we say that the destination is unreachable.

Consider the following figure to determine the hop count:

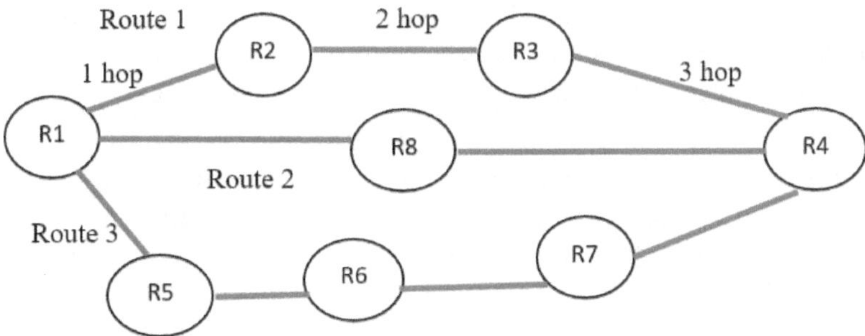

If R1 wants to send a packet to R4, it can go through R1 – R2 as 1 hop, R2 – R3 as 2 hop and R3-R4 as 3 hop.

In the above figure, if the packet has to go from R1 to R4, then it will choose the least number of hop counts.

Route 1 is from R1 – R2 – R3 – R4   = 3 hops

Route 2 is from R1 – R8 – R4   = 2 hops

Route 3 is from R1 – R5 – R6 – R7 – R8   = 4 hops

So Route 2 will be chosen, because it has the least 2 hops.

RIP Timers;

1) RIP Update Timer ; 30 seconds

The router attached with the RIP send their updates to all the neighbouring routers every 30 seconds.

2) RIP Invalid Timer : 180 seconds

In this if a network is disconnected and the link is down, then the neighbouring routers will wait 180 seconds for an update, if the update dose not arrive within 180 seconds, then it will mark it as unreachable.

3) RIP Flush Timer: 240 seconds

If the update is not received within 240 seconds, then that entry is removed from the routing table.

4.9.5 Open Shortest Path First (OSPF)

OSPF uses link state information for flooding and Dijkstra's least cost path algorithm. In OSPF, a router makes a graph of the whole Autonomous System. It then determines the shortest path to all smaller subnets using Dijkstra's Algorithm with itself being the root node. This information is broadcasted to all routers, not only the neighbouring ones. If there is any change in the cost up/down by any router, then the link state is broadcasted to all the routers. Also periodically after every 30 minutes, the link state is broadcasted even if there was no change.

An OSPF Autonomous System can be divided into Areas. Each Area is made up of Internal Routers. Each Area runs its own OSPF link state routing algorithm. Here each router in the Area broadcasts its link state to all the routers in that Area. In each Area, there are Area Border Routers, which have the responsibility of sending packets outside their Areas. There are Backbone Area Routers, which move packets between different Areas. A Boundary Router is used to exchange information to other Autonomous Systems.

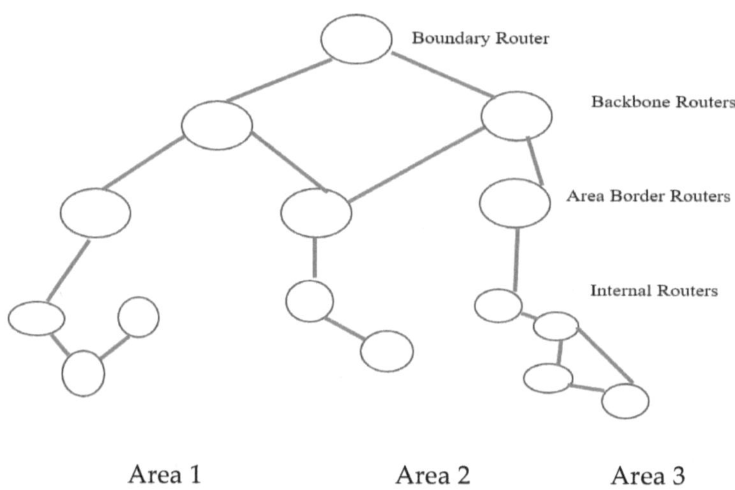

CHAPTER 5
THE DATA LINK LAYER

5.1 Introduction

The Link Layer lies beneath the network layer and is the layer which connects with the physical medium to pass the packets on the network. There can be two types of link layer activities

1) Broadcast channels used in LAN, WiFi. In this exists a common channel on which hosts are connected and then transmission can be coordinated and collisions avoided. A multiple access protocol is required to access this.

2) Point to Point link which exists between routers or between a dial-up-modem and ISP (Internet Service Provider).

The routers and hosts are referred to as nodes and the connection between the nodes is known as links. The packets that are passes on the links are known as frames. Each frame encapsulates the datagram passed from the upper network layer.

A link layer provides the following services:

1) Sending and Receiving frames

2) Error Detection

3) Retransmission

4) Flow Control

5) Random Access.

The link layer transfer of frames need not be done on the same types of link layer protocols or in other words a on one link may have ethernet, PPP on 2nd link and a WAN on 3rd link and so on.

Let us find out what are the functions of link layer:

1) Framing: A frame is formed by the header, trailer and data. The data comes simply from the upper layer (network layer). The addresses are put inside header and the error detecting bits in trailer.

2) Link Access: A Medium Access Control (MAC) protocol is used to specify the rules over which the transmission can be made.

3) Reliable Delivery: The link layer makes sure that the frames are delivered without loss. So it has acknowledgments and retransmissions.

4) Flow Control: The sender side and the receiver side have limited buffer capacity, so it ensures that the frames are not dropped after the buffer is full.

5) Error Detection: An error can be detected by finding out that a bit 1 is shown as a 0 or a bit 0 is shown as bit 1.

6) Error Correction: After the error is detected, it is known at which place the error occurred so that now we can correct it.

7) Half-Duplex Full-Duplex: Half-Duplex means that only one node can transmit at one time in either direction. Full-Duplex means that both nodes can transmit at the same time in either direction.

5.2 Error Detection and Correction

Three kinds of errors can occur:

1) Single Bit Error

2) Multiple Bits error

3) Burst Error

1) Single Bit Error:

In a frame, there is only one bit, anywhere though, which is corrupt.

2) Multiple Bits error

Frame is received with more than one bits in corrupted state.

3) Burst Error:

The sender send the data D and it is appended by error detection and correction bits (EDC). This EDC is completed on the whole frame containing the header fields and data sent from upper network layer. On the receiver side it gets D' and EDC' . The receiver knowing only D' and EDC' has to find out whether this contains the original D as the bits might have changed during transmission.

There are 3 ways in which it can be found out whether errors have been introduced or not.

    1) Parity Check

    2) Check Summing

    3) Cyclic Redundancy Check

Parity Check/Vertical Redundancy Check

This scheme uses a parity bit. Suppose we have data that consists of q bits. Then an additional parity bit (q+1) is chosen. The sender ensures that the number of 1s in the (q+1) bits (data + parity) is even.

The receiver counts the number of 1s in the received (q+1) bits. If odd number of 1s bits are found, then it can be seen as an error has occurred.

We say that system has even parity if the number of 1s in the data (data + parity) is even. We say that the system has odd parity if number of 1s in data (data + parity) is odd.

Suppose we have following data to be sent by sender

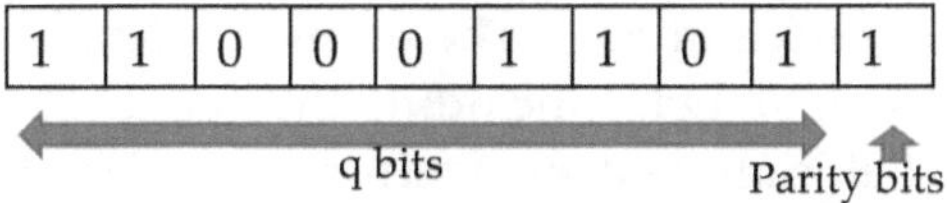

Suppose the receiver receives the same data as sent:

1 1 0 0 0 1 1 0 1 1

This is put in parity checker

If parity is even then it accepts it and if parity is odd then it rejects it.

2-Dimensional Parity Check /LRC or Longitudinal Redundancy Check

is also known as 2-D parity check.

The Data to be sent is arranged into table of rows and columns. The parity of each column is calculated and seen as a single row called redundant row. This row along with the original data is sent across. The receiver receives the data and the redundant row. Checks for any errors and then discards the redundant row.

Let us take an example,

Original Data to send

11001100   11011010   11100100   10001001

Arranged in a table

               1 1 0 0 1 1 0 0
               1 1 0 1 1 0 1 0
               1 1 1 0 0 1 0 0
               1 0 0 0 1 0 0 1
Taking XOR   ------------------------
Redundant Row   0 1 1 1 1 0 1 1

Receiver Receives:

11001100   11011010   11100100   10001001   0 1 1 1 1 0 1 1

←—————————— Original Data ————————→   Parity Bits/Redundant Row

Checksum Method

The data is taken as 16 bit integers and they are summed up. Then the 1's complement of the sum is taken and it becomes the internet checksum. And this value is inserted in the checksum field of the header (remember this is the header of TCP / UDP segment) and sent across. When we were calculating the checksum, the checksum field of the header was all 0s. After calculating the checksum, this value is inserted in the header checksum field. The receiver calculates whether there is any error or not. So it sums up all fields including the header checksum and then takes 1's complement. If all fields are 1s then no error, if any filed has 0, then an error has occurred.

Cyclic Redundancy Check

Cyclic Redundancy Check is based on binary division. Here we have data which is n bits to send . We take key k bits, which we use as divisor or the number with which division is to be made. We add k-1 zero bits to the n bits so that the data elongates. At each step we XOR the bits with the divisor. The remainder found is known as the CRC or Cyclic Redundancy Check. So our new data to send becomes (data +CRC). At the receiver side we get the data which is (data +CRC). We use the same key k to divide. We perform the division as we did on sender's side. If the remainder is all 0s then we say no transmission error. If we have non zero remainder then we say transmission error has occurred.

Let us take an example to explain, Suppose we have

Data (n bits) to send = 100100

Key (k bits) (Divisor) = 1101

Add k-1 bits of zeros to data = 000

New data becomes (n + k-1 0s) = 100100000

Performing Division:

```
1101 | 100100000
       1101
       --------------------
        01000
        1101
       --------------------
         01010
         1101
       --------------------
          01110
          1101
       --------------------
           00110
           000
       --------------------
            1100
            1101
       ----------------
            0001
```

So our remainder is 001 (CRC)

Receiver Side Received (Data + CRC)

Which is 100100 + 001

So new data becomes 100100001

Performing division with same key k which is 1101

```
1101 | 100100001
       1101
       --------------------
        01000
        1101
       --------------------
         01010
         1101
       --------------------
          01110
          1101
       --------------------
```

                    00110

                    0000

                    1101

                    1101

          0000(Remainder All zeros means accepted)

Let us suppose there was some transmission error and we received our data as 100000001

performing division with same key (1101)

          1101 | 100000001

                    1101

                    01010

                    1101

                    01110

                    1101

                    00110

                    0000

                    1100

                    1101

                    00011

                    0000

          011(Remainder not all zeros , therefore rejected)

5.3 Multiple Access Protocol

The network links are of two types:

1) Point to Point Link

2) Broadcast Link

In Point to Point Link, there is a single sender and a single receiver connected to each other on the link. In a broadcast link, there may be multiple senders and multiple receivers connected to each other on a single common broadcast channel.

In a broadcast one machine sends the packet and all other machines on the channel receive it. The example of such a network are ethernet and the wired LAN. In this approach more than 2 stations can send packets at the same time. So if that happens then we say a collision has occurred. In collision, none of the stations can do any useful work, the frames are simple discarded. If the broadcast channel has to work properly then the nodes need to coordinate with each other as to how to send the frames.

The multiple access protocols are of three types:

   1) Channel Partitioned

   2) Random Access

   3) Taking Turns

5.3.1 Channel Partitioning Protocol

We had studied in the first chapter regarding Time Division Multiplexing (TDM) and Frequency Division Multiplexing (FDM). TDM eliminates collision as each node gets a dedicated transmission rate. The drawback of TDM is that the rate of transmission is always R/N. For each node R is the rate and N the number of nodes. And also the node has to wait for its turn to come. Then FDM is a better option than TDM where frequency bands are reserved for transmission.

5.3.2 Random Access Protocols

In this protocol, a transmitting node always transmits at the full rate of the channel say R mbps. On colliding, the frames does not retransmit immediately. Rather it waits a random delay before re transmitting. Each node chooses a different random delay, with this they back off with a different random time and then retransmit after that random time.

<u>ALOHA</u>

This is one of the simple types of carrier sense multiple access protocol.

<u>Slotted ALOHA</u>

In slotted ALOHA, the following considerations are made:

   1) All the frames have the same number of bits say L.

   2) Slots are made by dividing the time in size of L/R seconds. Which means one frame is transmitted in 1 time slot only.

   3) The transmission takes place at the beginning of the slot.

   4) The nodes are synchronized to know where a slot begins.

   5) If a collision takes place in a slot then, all other slots come to know about it before the slot ends.

p is a probability between 0 and 1. If a new frame needs to be sent, then it will wait till the beginning of the time slot occurs. If there is no collision then there is no retransmission. If there is a collision then retransmission takes place with a probability p.

Slotted ALOHA performs best when there is only one active node. It does not however perform well when there are multiple active nodes. In case of multiple active nodes, a small fraction of slots will experience collision and that is wasted time. And yet another fraction of time all the nodes will refrain from sending if there is a collision.

Node 1								
Node 2								
Node 3								
	Collision	Empty	Collision	Sending	Collision	Empty	Sending	Sending

In the above diagram you can see there are 3 nodes which collide in slot 1, then 2nd slot is empty. At slot 3 node 1 and node 3 collide again. At 4th slot node 1 is sending. At 5th slot node 2 and node 3 collide again. At slot 6th, it is empty. At slot 7, node 2 is sending and at slot 8, node 3 is sending.

Pure ALOHA

In Slotted ALOHA, the requirement is to synchronize all nodes so that they transmit at the beginning of the slot. In pure ALOHA when a frame arrives from the upper network layer. The frame is immediately transmitted on the broadcast channel. If a collision occurs, the frame is will be retransmitted after a probability p. In other words we can say at any given time the frame is retransmitted with a probability p and waits for another free time with probability (1-p).

Carrier Sense Multiple Access

In pure ALOHA and slotted ALOHA, when a node begins to transmit, it does not pay attention to any other node transmitting at that time. And also the node does not stop transmission if there is interference from another node transmitting.

So we include the term carrier sense. Carrier sense means that before transmitting, you take a look at the broadcasting channel to see if there is any frame which is currently being transmitted. That means we listen to the channel before transmitting. If a node is currently transmitting onto the channel, then the node "backs off" a random amount of time and then again senses the channel before transmitting. The frame will only be transmitted if the channel is idle and there is no activity on it.

If both nodes begin to transmit at the same time after seeing the channel that it was idle for both of them, then we say collision takes place, this is known as collision detection. As the nodes detect that the transmission is going on before sending their own frames, the chances of collision are reduced.

There are 3 types of CSMA

    1) I Persistence

    2) Non Persistence

    3) P -Persistent

I – Persistent : In this method the station continuously monitors the network, if it is busy, then the station waits until it is idle. In case the channel is idle, it immediately transmits the frame with the probability of 1. And hence it is called I – persistent

This method has the highest chances that a collision will occur. Because if 2 or more frames sense that the channel is idle , they both transmit at the same time. When a collision occurs, they back off and wait a random amount of time to start all over again.

Non_Persistent : In this method the station does not monitor the channel continuously. If a station wants to transmit a frame, it will sense the channel, if it is busy, it will wait a fixed amount of time and check again. If it finds the channel is still busy, it will again wait, If it finds the channel idle, then it transmits the frame immediately.

P-Persistent: If the station finds the channel idle, it may or may not send. If the channel is idle, the station will transmit with a probability p and wait with a probability (1-p). This is used in slotted ALOHA, with a probability of (1-p), it waits for the next time slot. If the next time slot is idle, it sends with a probability p. p is calculated as follows:

$P = (1 - 1/N)^{N-1}$

Where N is the number of stations connected to the channel

Eg – say there are 5 stations, and station 1 wants to transmit

$P = 0.4096 ((1-1/5)^4)$,

It will transmit until 0.4096

And wait till (1-0.4096)

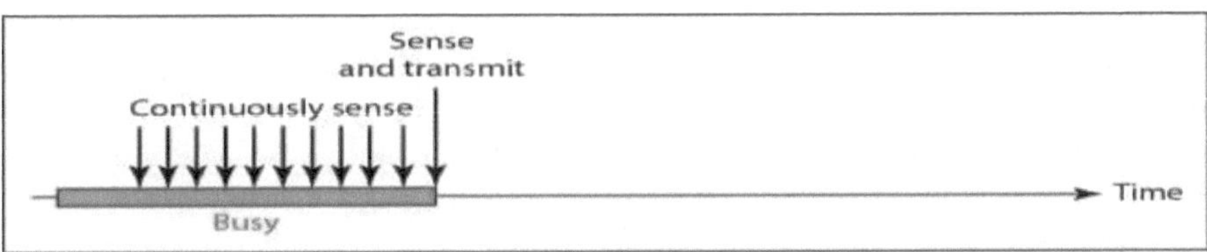

a. 1-persistent

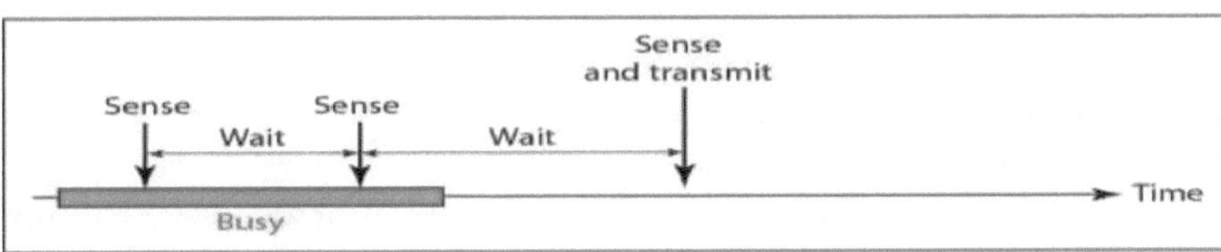

b. Nonpersistent

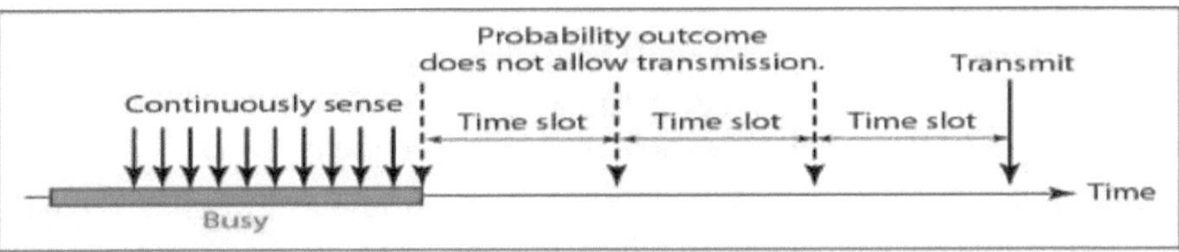

c. p-persistent

<u>CSMA/CD (Carrier Sense with Multiple Access/Collision Detect)</u>

Carrier sense with collision detect is explained below in Ethernet.

CSMA/CA(Carrier Sense with Multiple Access/Collision Avoidance)

Collision avoidance is achieved with a backoff factor. A station senses whether the channel is idle or not. If it is idle, it will send the frame. If it is not idle, a random period of time is chosen as the backoff factor. A counter is attached to the backoff factor. It waits till backoff factor counter becomes zero. After that the whole process is started again.

5.3.3 Taking Turns Protocol

An example of a taking turn protocol is token passing protocol. In this protocol there is no master slave relationship. A special purpose frame known as token is used to give access to the node. This token is passed to the nodes in a specific order. For example, if node 1 passes token to node 2, then node 2 passes to node 3and so on. The node that receives the token has the authority to send frames where all other nodes will be receiving the sent frame. If a node receives the token and it does not have anything to transmit, then it will pass token to next node.

The disadvantage with this is that if a node becomes unfunctional, then the whole channel is broken and we cannot have other nodes using tokens.

5.4 MAC (Media Access Control) Addresses

In networks, we use 2 types of addresses, IP addresses and MAC Addresses. The network layer deals with IP addresses and the link layer deals with MAC addresses also called physical addresses.

The MAC addresses are 6 bytes long. Which is 6*8 = 48 bits. So the maximum number of possible physical addresses can be 2^{48}. These addresses are expressed hexadecimal notation and each byte is expressed as a pair of hexadecimal number. These are separated by hyphens. An example is as follows:

12-4F-A1-B5-01-22

The MAC addresses are permanent in nature. This address is given by the manufacturer and burned on the Network Interface Card (NIC). The MAC address remains the same wherever it goes. If you are in India or America the MAC address will not change and remain the same.

An IP address changes as we move from one place to another. So if a computer has a particular IP address in India and then he travels to America, then its IP address will also change.

When a frame is received from the upper network layer, the link layer puts the Source MAC address and the destination MAC address in the header field and encapsulates the frame with header field and passes to the network.

If the underlying technology is a LAN broadcast just as Ethernet, then all the nodes receive this frame. The node which has the MAC address same as the one in destination field acquires the frame, detaches the header field and passes on the remaining frame to its upper level protocol layer in the TCP/IP stack. All other nodes had also received this frame but they discarded it as the MAC address in the destination field did not match with their MAC address.

5.5 Address Resolution Protocol (ARP)

The IP addresses are mapped to physical addresses so that source and destination nodes can be identified on the network.

Let us take an example, suppose we have the following nodes:

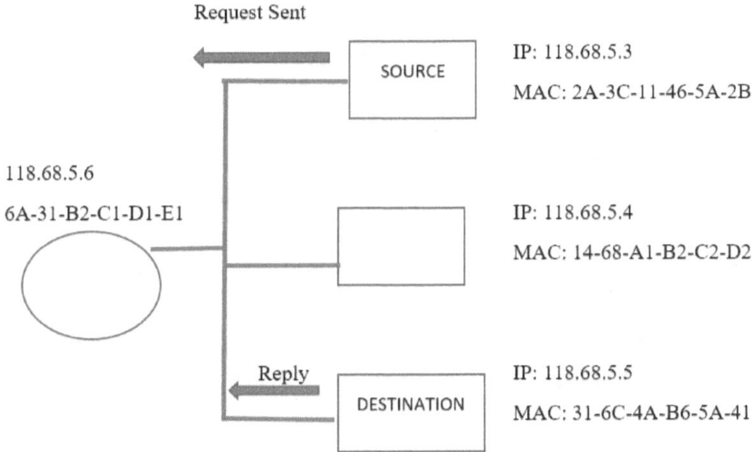

The node 118.68.5.3 wants to send a frame to 118.68.5.5.

Both the source and destination are on same network. The source node must have both IP address and the MAC address of the destination so that it can build the header of the frame and send it into the LAN.

Now the question comes that how does the source come to know of the destination's MAC address. It has its own source IP address, source MAC address and the destination's IP address passed from upper layer. Referring to our example, how can source node with IP 118.68.5.3 and MAC 2A-3C-11-46-5A-2B come to know the MAC address of Destination with IP 118.68.5.5.

This is where ARP is used. It takes as input the IP address and return as output the corresponding MAC address mapped onto its LAN.

So in our example, the Source 118.68.5.3 sends an ARP frame who's input is the IP address 118.68.5.5. and this returns the MAC address as output 31-6C-4A-B6-5A-41. So now the source has both IP address of Source and destination and MAC addresses of both source and destination.

How does ARP work

Each node (host and router) has an ARP table stored in RAM. The ARP table consists of the mapping between the IP addresses and their corresponding mapped

MAC addresses. If the sending node has an ARP entry of the destination node in its ARP table, then it can see the destination MAC address from there. If the table entry does not exist, then an ARP query frame is built with the IP address of the destination node and broadcasted onto the channel. The node having the matching IP address returns the reply with the corresponding MAC address. The other nodes simply discard the request since they see that the destination IP is not their's. The sender then updates its ARP table and proceeds further.

IP ADDRESS	MAC ADDRESS
118.68.5.3	2A-3C-11-46-5A-2B
118.68.5.4	14-68-A1-B2-C2-D2
118.68.5.5	31-6C-4A-B6-5A-41

ARP TABLE

RARP (Reverse Address Resolution Protocol)

Reverse Address Resolution Protocol as the name suggest does the opposite of ARP. As in ARP we know the IP address and we want the corresponding MAC address. In This we have the MAC address and we want the corresponding IP address.

This is used in the case nodes are trying to find their IP addresses dynamically. Or we have a new machine which is set up on the network and wants to know its IP address.

The network system administrator creates a table in the RARP server which holds the mapping of MAC addresses to their IP addresses.

How does RARP work?

A device connects to the LAN and sends an RARP packet containing the MAC address to all nodes on the broadcast channel. Here Physical address is sent and request is made to return its IP address. All nodes receive the request package but they simple discard it because they are not the RARP server. Hence the RARP server accepts the request, looks up its table and sends back the corresponding IP address.

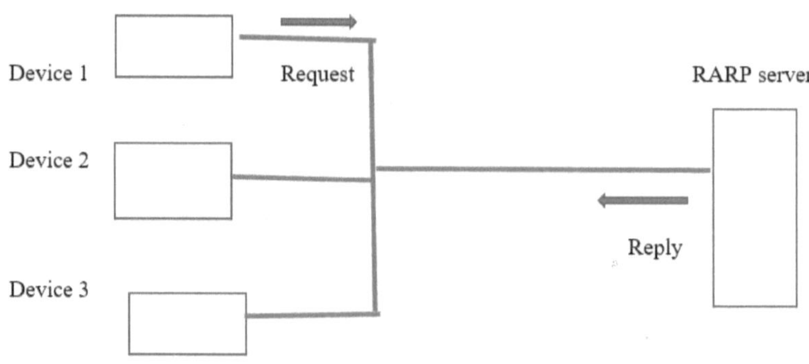

5.6 Dynamic Host Configuration Protocol (DHCP)

This protocol assigns IP addresses dynamically to the hosts. It is based on client server architecture. If a host on a client wants to configure network information, then a DHCP server needs to be present in each subnet. If a DHCP server is not there, then a DHCP relay agent which knows the address of a DHCP server will be enough for configuration.

The DHCP works as follows:

1) The very first thing that a client needs to do is to find out the DHCP server with which it can interact. A DHCP discover message is sent using UDP packet to port 67. The UDP packet is a transport layer protocol, the underlying network layer does not have the IP address to which it can send the frame. The host does not have an IP address of the network and neither has an IP address of the DHCP server. The DHCP client generates an IP datagram with the DHCP Discover message inside it. It uses the broadcast address 255.255.255.255 (destination) and source address 0.0.0.0 (for itself) and passes the datagram on the network. The broadcast message is received by everyone. If a DHCP server receives it, then it replies to the host using a transaction ID field of the DHCP request. If a DHCP relay agent receives it then it forwards the message to the DHCP server.

2) The server replies back to the client by giving a DHCP offer message. This offer contains the transaction ID to identify which request did it come from. The datagram sent back is a UDP segment containing DHCP offer message, the transaction ID and the proposed IP address, the subnet mask and the IP address lease time.

3) The client then chooses from a number of server offer messages and again replies back to the chosen server by sending back the configuration parameters.

4) The server replies back to the DHCP request message by sending a DHCP acknowledgement message and confirms the requested parameters.

Once a DHCP acknowledgement is received, the client uses the DHCP allocated IP address for the given lease time. It can further renew the lease time if it is getting over.

DHCP CLIENT

DHCP SERVER

221.6.7.2

DHCP Discover

Src: 0.0.0.0

Dest: 255.255.255.255:67

DHCP Discover

ipaddr:0.0.0.0

Transaction ID :125

DHCP offer

←——————————————————————————————————

Src: 221.6.7.2
Dest: 255.255.255.255:68
DHCP offer
ipaddr:221.6.7.3
Transaction ID :125
DHCP server IP: 221.6.7.2
Lease time : 2400 s

DHCP Request

——————————————————————————————————→

Src:0.0.0.0

Dest:255.255.25.255:67

DHCP Request

ipaddr: 221.6.7.3

Transaction ID :126

DHCP server: 221.6.7.2

Lease time/:2400 s

DHCP Acknowledgement

←——————————————————————————————————

Src: 221.6.7.2.
Dest: 255.255.255.255:68
DHCP Acknowledgement
ipaddr:221.6.7.3
Transaction ID;126
DHCP server: 221.6.7.2
Lease time: 2400 s

In the above diagram, the IP address offered is 221.6.7.3 by the server.

5.7 Bootstrap Protocol (BOOTP)

Now that we have talked about DHCP, let us also mention BOOTP. Both BOOTP and DHCP are used to get the IP addresses of machines. BOOTP uses limited broadcast address (255.255.255.255) while asking for IP address. The major difference between BOOTP and DHCP is that BOOTP is used to get IP addresses of machines that are static, while DHCP is used to get the IP addresses of machines that are dynamic in nature or in other words mobile devices.

Whenever a network machine boots up, it requests an IP address from the BOOTP server. The BOOTP server sends back an IP address from the pool of addresses provided by the administrator. BOOTP supports only manual configuration whereas DHCP automatically gets and allocates IP addresses. BOOTP does not allocate temporary IP addresses whereas DHCP allocates temporary IP addresses and also for a short duration of time. BOOTP may cause errors because of manual configuration whereas DCHP is less prone to errors because of automatic configuration.

5.8 Internet Control Message Protocol (ICMP)

ICMP is a used for notifying the sender of any error that has occurred. This is because there is no built in protocol for error detection. This protocol is used by hosts and routers to report of any error or send control messages. The IP packet carries the IP address of the source and destination. The packet on passing through intermediate routers does not have the address of the router, therefore the error message can only be sent back to the source IP address. An ICMP message is put in the IP datagram.

The IP datagram looks like this:

The ICMP Message is further broken down as follows:

0	7	15	31
8 bit type	8 bit code	16 bit checksum	

The 8 bit types tells the type of message

The 8 bit code tells more information of the type

The 16 bit checksum contains the ICMP message.

Some common examples of ICMP messages include:

   a) Host not reachable

   b) Any message sent which is bigger than the receiver capacity.

Some examples of 8 bit Type are as follows:

Type 0 - Echo a Reply

Type 8 – Echo a Request

Type 3 – Destination Unreachable

Type 5 – Redirect a Message

Type 11 – Time Exceeded

Type 12 – Parameter Problem

Below are given some 8 code bits with 8 type bits for clarification:

Type	Code	Description
0	0	Echo a Reply
3	0	Destination Network not reachable
3	1	Destination host not reachable
3	2	Destination Protocol not reachable
3	3	Destination Port not reachable
5	0	Redirect the datagram for the network
5	1	Redirect the datagram for the host
5	2	Redirect the datagram for service and network
5	3	Redirect the datagram for service and host
8	0	Echo a Request
11	0	Time to Live exceeded while in transit
11	1	Time of fragment reassembly exceded.
12	1	Missing a required option field
12	2	Length not correct

There are number of denial of service attacks from which the ICMP has to recover, they are as follows, In denial of service the target machine is bombarded with large number of packets, so that the machine becomes dysfunctional.

A) Ping of Death Attack: In this a ping message is sent of size much greater than the maximum allowable size. So it needs to be broken into smaller units. On reassembling the buffer is overloaded and then the machine gives up.

B) ICMP flood attack: In this a large number of ping messages are sent together, which causes the machine to give up.

C) Smurf Attack: In this the attacker sends ICMP messages via IP spoofing. IP spoofing means a false IP address is used so that someone tries to impersonate another person.

Some other messages that ICMP uses are as follows:

1) Source Quench Message: When a destination machine detects that the rate of sending is much more than the rate of receiving,

then it sends a source quench message to sender for slowing down the transmission rate.

2) Time Exceeded: When a packet has travelled the network through routers and still has not reached its destination, then its time to live field reaches a value of zero. Then ICMP extracts the source IP address and sends a time exceeded message to the source.

3) Fragmentation Required: When the packet size is large and Do Not Fragment bit is set, then a router sends a message to the source indicating that the destination is unreachable and fragmentation is required.

4) Destination Unreachable: When a packet is not able to reach its destination due to the following reasons:

   a) Destination Machine is down

   b) A router in between is not able to forward packets

   c) A firewall is deployed and does allow packets to pass

   Then a message is sent to the source.

5) Redirect Message: When a router comes to know about a shorter path to destination is possible, then it informs the source about it.

5.9 Ethernet

Ethernet is the most prevalent LAN technology. The structure of the Ethernet is as follows:

Preamble	Destination Address	Source Address	Type	Payload (Data)	CRC

The payload field contains the IP datagram. Suppose both source and destination machines are on the same Ethernet LAN. Then Ethernet would require the source MAC address and the destination MAC address and pass the frame to the physical layer for transmission. The receiving node receives the frame from the physical layer, extracts the IP datagram and passes to the upper network layer.

1) Data field: contains IP datagram whose length is 1500 bytes. If the IP datagram is more than 1500 bytes, then fragmentation is required.

2) Destination address: MAC address of destination machine

3) Source Address: MAC address of source machine.

4) Type field: This field tells us the network layer protocol that has been used. It may be other than IP. This field is similar to protocol field in the network layer protocol.

5) Cyclic Redundancy Check (CRC): This is used to detect whether error have occurred or not.

6) Preamble: These bits are used to synchronize the clock. The first 7 bytes contain 10101010 and the last eighth byte contains 10101011. The last 2 bits 11 indicate that important stuff is coming.

The Ethernet is an unreliable service. If the CRC field fails, then no negative acknowledgement is given back and if the CRC passes then also no positive acknowledgement is given.

<u>CSMA/CD Ethernet multiple access protocol</u>

The nodes on the Ethernet are able to sense the channel when another nodes are transmitting. This helps them to find out that a collision has occurred. Each node runs its own CSMA/CD protocol without coordinating with other nodes. CSMA/CD is carried out as follows:

1) The host gets the network layer datagram, prepares the Ethernet frame and puts the frame in the buffer.

2) The host senses that the channel is idle, then it transmits the frame. If it finds that the channel is busy, it waits until it finds that the channel is idle (by checking the signal energy).

3) While transmitting, it still checks the signal energy, if no signal energy is detected, it transmits the frame successfully.

4) If it detects a signal energy, it stops transmission and it sends a jam signal. The jam signal is 48 bits in length.

5) After stopping transmission, it enters an exponential backoff phase.

5.10 High Level Data Link Control Protocol (HDLC)

This is a bit oriented protocol which operates at the data link layer of the protocol, which is used to communicate between point to point and multipoint communication. The communication takes by sending frames from source to destination. This protocol provides many functionalities such as framing, error correction, error detection and flow control. There are primary and secondary computers which send and receive frames.

There are two modes of communication:

1) Normal Mode

This is used for communication between multipoint and point to point communication. Suppose we send a frame from a primary computer, this is known as sending a command, the secondary computer then receives the command and responds back by sending a response. If multipoint is used then all secondary computers send back their responses.

2) Asynchronous mode

This is used for only point to point communication.

All computers are allowed to send commands and receive responses.

Normal Mode Point to Point

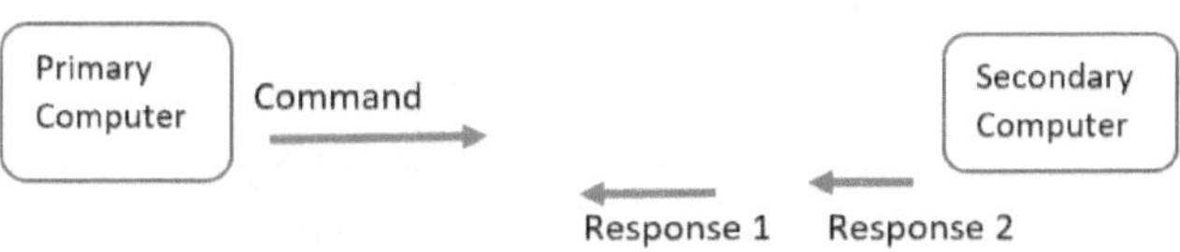

Normal Mode Multi Point

Asynchronous Mode

The HDLC contains the following frame format:

Flag	Address	Control	Payload	FCS	Flag
1 byte	1 byte	1 byte	variable bytes	2 or 4 bytes	1 byte

1) Flag : This has an 8 bits which contain the value (01111110). This is used at the beginning and at the end to distinguish from where the frame starts and frame ends.

2) Address: If the primary computer is sending a command, then the address contains the address of secondary computer where it has to be delivered. On the other hand, if the secondary computer is sending a response, then the address contains the address of the primary computer where it has to be delivered.

3) Control: This has a value of either 0 or 1, to indicate flow control or error control.

4) Payload : This is the data passed from the upper network layer.

5) FCS: This is the frame check sequence which is used for error detection. The algorithm used is Cyclic Redundancy Check(CRC).

5.11 Routers Switches Hubs

The routers, hubs and switches are used to inter connect the LANs.

A hub is the simplest device which is used for interconnection. A hub connects the devices in a point to point manner. There can be backbone hubs which further connect to normal hubs. By interconnecting the hubs, we increase the range or the distance of travel is extended. A hub is mainly a repeater, it does not have any storage capacity or buffer. It operates at the physical layer of the TCP/IP protocol stack. A hub can join only same type of underlying technologies such as 10BaseT.

A switch operates at the link layer level of the protocol or they operate at ethernet frames. Switches forward the frames on the LAN. A LAN could have been constructed by different underlying technologies such as 10BaseT, 100BaseT or Gigabit Ethernet.

Switches perform 2 major functionalities:

1) Forwarding

2) Filtering

In filtering the switch decides whether the frame has to be forwarded or dropped. In forwarding the switch decides which interface should the frame be forwarded to. The above is achieved with the help of a switch table. A switch table consists of the following entries:

1) The MAC address of the node

2) The Interface which leads to the node

3) The time the entry was made in the switch table

Address	Interface	Time
1A-23-AB-CD-24-34	1	8:56
23-2B-2C-3D-34-56	3	8:59

There are two possibilities:

1) The MAC address is in the switch table

2) The MAC address is not in the switch table

Suppose a frame with destination address 1A-23-AB-CD-24-34 arrives at the switch from interface 1. On examining the switch table the switch comes to know that the interface to forward is also interface 1, so this is just a broadcast and hence no need to forward, just filter and drop the frame. Now consider another scenario that the frame came from interface 2 and had the same destination address as 1A-23-AB-CD-24-34. On seeing the switch table this needs to be forwarded to interface 1, so the switch just forwards the frame to interface 1.

A hub does not bother to see whether a signal is there on the LAN. It just simply finds bits for transmission. The switch on the other hand uses the CSMA/CD algorithm to find out whether there is signal energy on the channel or not. The switch uses exponential backoff in case a collision occurs. The switch is not associated with MAC addresses (the host or router used to insert MAC addresses before sending). The switch does not change the source address of the frame.

The switch possesses a special property known as self learning. The switch table is built dynamically at run time and also automatically without the support of the network administrator or the configuration protocol. Self learning is achieved as follows:

1) At first the switch table is empty.

2) When a frame arrives on one interface of the switch and the destination MAC address of the frame is not present in the switch table, a copy is sent to the output buffer.

3) The switch then stores in its table the MAC address of the source's address field, the interface from which it came and the current time. This way the switch keeps on learning the interface from which the MAC address came.

4) When a frame comes who's destination address is in the switch table entry, then it forwards that frame to the respective interface.

5) There is an age limit that is assigned to each table entry. Each entry is given a time to exist in the table say 50 minutes. If an entry has not been referred to for the given time then it is deleted from the switch table. Suppose interface 1 with destination address 1A-23-AB-CD-24-34 has been residing in the table for 50 minutes and has not been referred. Then the switch will delete this entry from its table.

Switches have another property known as plug and play. This means switches can be attached to the network any time, work with it and then removed without needing any network administrator or any configuration protocol.

The routers are known as store and forward devices. The routers work at the internet layer of the TCP/IP protocol stack and are called layer-3 devices. Switches are plug and play so they do packet switching and filtering at higher rates. The switches are not capable to handle broadcast storms. A broadcast storm takes place if one node goes out of control and keeps transmitting packets into the channel till the time that the channel is completely blocked. The routers have a firewall protection against the broadcast storms. The routers take more time than switches because they process at one layer higher than the switches i.e. the internet layer or network layer. The routers are considered intelligent because they can take different routes according to the fact that which route is the best at this point of time. If another route is best at another time then they will take that.

5.12 Reliable Data Transfer Protocols

TCP is a reliable protocol, but the layer below the TCP is IP which is unreliable. So it is the responsibility of TCP to deliver packets in order and all of them. If something goes wrong then TCP has to take care of it. The data that is sent from the sender to receiver is unidirectional.

When we make transmissions over the network, we want to have some kind of indication from the receiver that so far so good. Because if we blindly send all the data and find out in the end that something went wrong after 2nd packet, then all our efforts will go waste. So we need a mechanism where the receiver either sends a positive acknowledgement saying that ii is ok or a negative acknowledgement that please resend. To implement reliable transfer, we need 2 things:

1) Detecting that an error occurred by checksum method

2) Feedback from the receiver, positive feedback to say do not repeat and negative feedback to say send again.

Here we will now consider the following points:

1) If an acknowledgement is lost

2) If acknowledgement is lost and sender resends then duplicate packets problem will come

3) The receiver will not know if it was a new message or a retransmission

The solution to the above is to put a sequence number in the field. Then the receiver simply checks sequence number and behaves accordingly.

5.12.1 Stop and Wait Protocol

We use checksums, sequence numbers, acknowledgements and retransmissions to do our work.

The sender sends the packet and waits for its acknowledgement, and if a positive acknowledgement comes it sends the second packet. So how much time should it wait to get an acknowledgement and then retransmit again. So it should decide an appropriate time limit that it should wait before resending. So we put a countdown timer which if expires then we send the data again.

The following situations may arise

1) A normal transmission

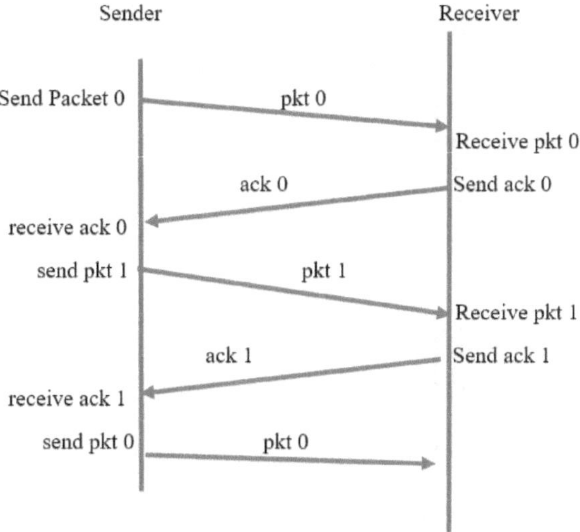

so it alternates between the pkt0 and pkt1. It waits for an acknowledgement to come before sending the next packet. So no sequence numbers are used here.

2) Suppose our packet is lost

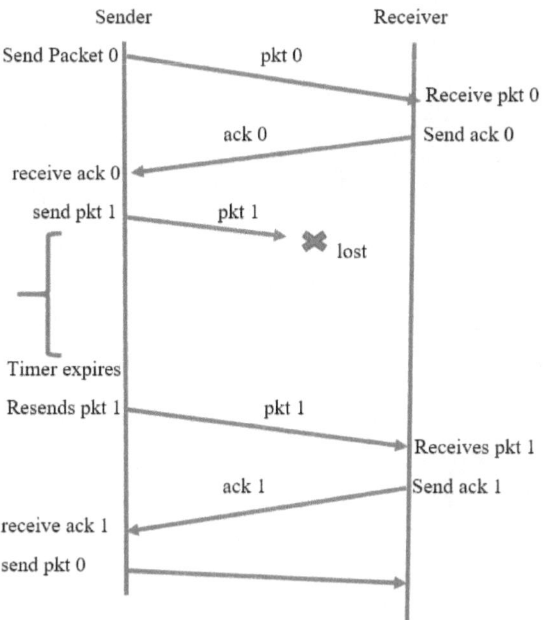

3) Suppose our Acknowledgement is lost

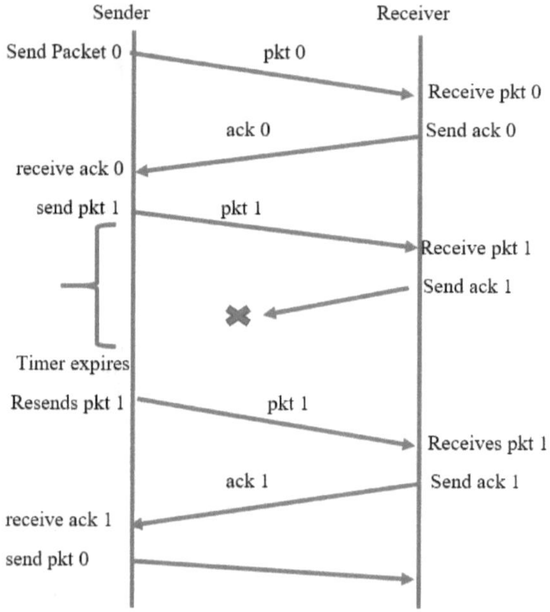

4) If Acknowledgments is delayed

If the acknowledgement is delayed then, it can be wrongly considered as the acknowledgement of some other packet, and meanwhile the timer expires, so the frame is transmitted again. At the receiver side the frame is discarded as it is duplicate.

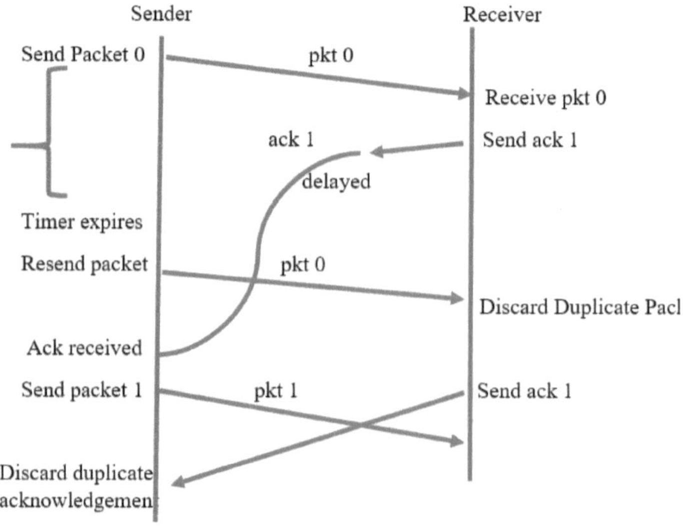

The stop and wait protocol waits too much before sending the packets so we introduce pipelining protocols, which send multiple packets in one go without waiting for acknowledgements. The sender and receiver both buffer more than one packet. This is done by two techniques called:

1) Go Back N

2) Selective Repeat

5.12.2 Go Back N

Here we use sequence numbers to send. A window size of N is defined which contains the range of permissible sequence numbers for transmission but which have not yet been acknowledged, The window slides over the sequence number space and this is known as sliding window protocol.

The size of window on senders side is N whereas the receivers window size is 1. If there are corrupted frames, then they are discarded also out of order frames are also discarded.

If the acknowledgements are not received, then retransmission of all the frames in the current window are retransmitted.

Suppose a window contains 14 frames to be transmitted, their sequence numbers are from 0 to 13. Our window size is 4, which means at one time 4 frames can be sent together before receiving acknowledgment of 1st frame.

13 12 11 10 9 8 7 6 5 4 3 2 1 0

Current window 0 1 2 3

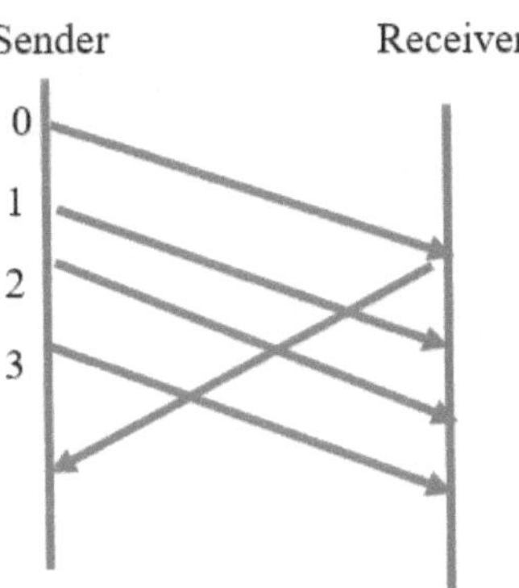

13 12 11 10 9 8 7 6 5 | 4 3 2 1 | 0

Current window 1 2 3 4

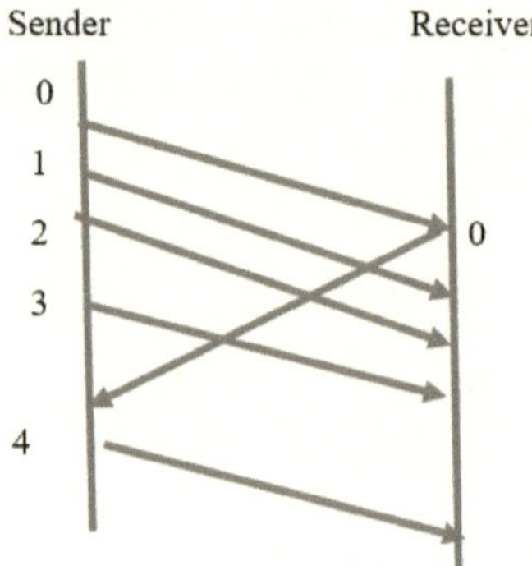

13 12 11 10 9 8 7 6 | 5 4 3 2 | 1 0

Current window 2 3 4 5

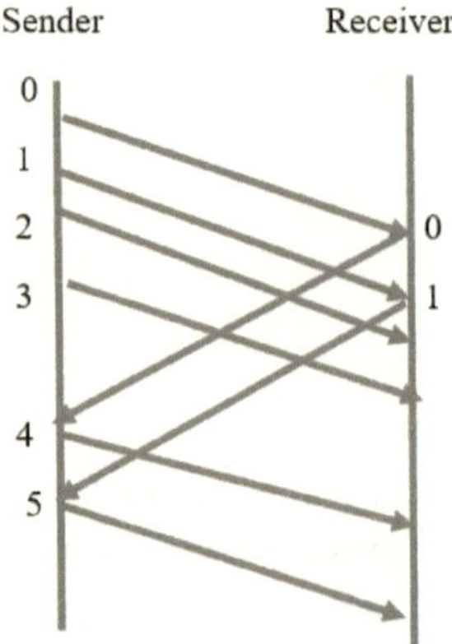

Now Suppose Ack 2 is lost

13 12 11 10 9 8 7 6 | 5 4 3 2 | 1 0

Current window 2 3 4 5

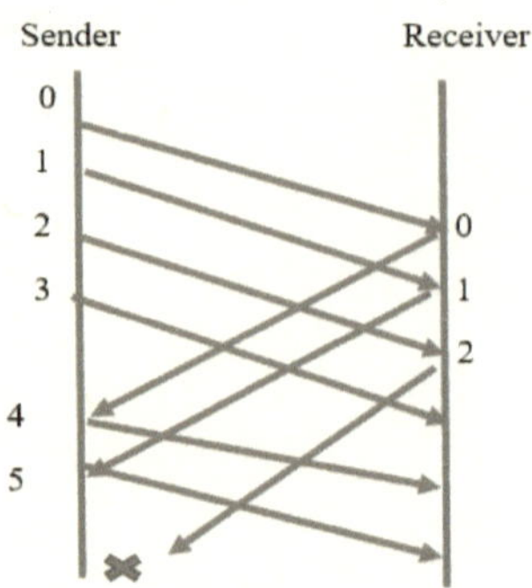

If Ack 2 is lost, then the entire current window is sent again. i.e. 2 3
4 5

13 12 11 10 9 8 7 6 $\boxed{5\ 4\ 3\ 2}$ 1 0

Current window 2 3 4 5   Sender   Receiver

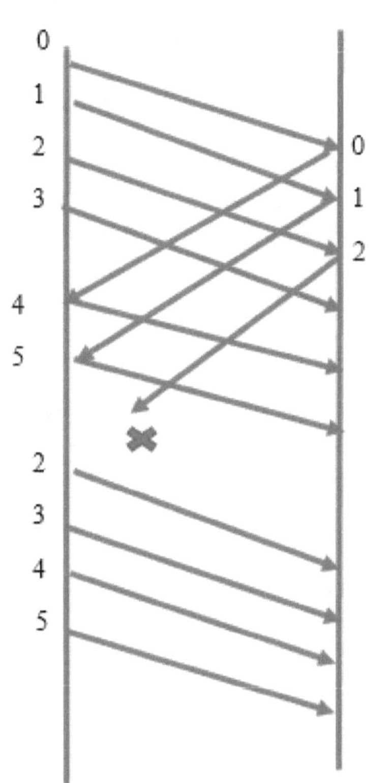

In Go Back N scheme, we retransmit all the frames in the current window if an acknowledgement has been lost. And we go back N, means we go to the number N from where the current sliding window is starting. In this case the active current sliding window was from 2 to 5 , so we go back to the number 2 and transmit all frames in the current slider which are 2, 3, 4 and 5.

5.12.3 Selective Repeat ARQ

In selective repeat ARQ, retransmission of frames take place which are arriving out of sequence. Which means frames which are either lost or have been corrupted. The correct frames are put into a buffer. The receiver keeps track of all the sequence numbers of the correctly arrived frames and sends acknowledgements.

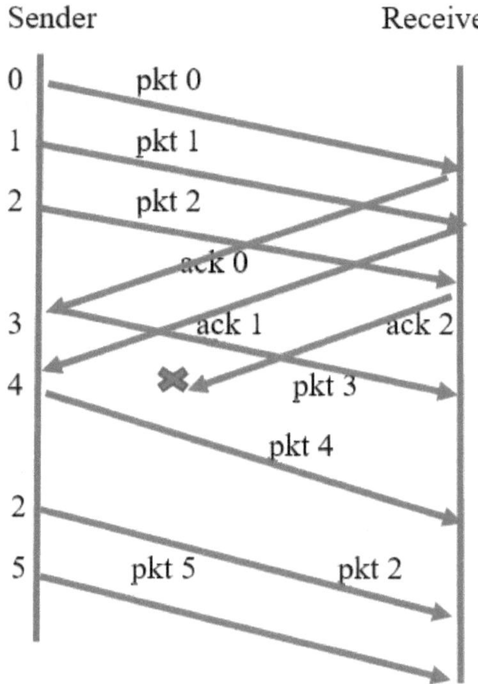

Here only packet 2 is transmitted again, because only packet 2s acknowledgement was not received.

APPENDIX

SOLVED PROBLEMS

Q1. What is the transmission time of a packet sent by a station if the length of the packet is 2 million bytes and the bandwidth of the channel is 300kbps

Ans: Transmission time = (packet length)/(bandwidth)

$$= 2\text{million bytes} / 300\text{kbps}$$

$$= 2000000 * 8 \text{ bits} / 300000 \text{ bps}$$

$$= 53.33 \text{ s}$$

Q2. What is the propagation delay if the packet is sent through an optic fibre with the propagation speed of 2.1 x 10^8 m/s and the distance between the source and destination is 5000 km.

Ans: Propagation time = distance / speed

$$= 5 \times 10^6 / 2.1 \times 10^8$$

$$= 0.0238 \text{ s}$$

Q3. Subnet mask 255.255.248.0 find max no host –

Ans: No of 1 in mask=21(n)

11111111.11111111.11111000.00000000

max no host = 2^{32-21} -2

$$= 2^{11} -2$$

$$= 2046$$

Q4. What is the net mask of the gateway interface in a subnetwork where maximum of 25 hosts exist andip address of one of the hosts is 192:168:1:1?

Ans: For 25 host we require 5-bits reserve for host.

This means prefix length is /27(27continious 1's followed by all 0's).

11111111.11111111.11111111.11100000

So net mask is 255.255.255.224.

Q5. An IP router has a maximum transfer unit of 1500 bytes with 20 bytes as header and 4434 bytes received. Show the fragments, their offset values and values in more fragment bits.

Ans: Total data that needs to be sent is 4434-20 = 4414

Data that can be sent in 1 go is 1500-20 = 1480

No of fragments required are 4414/1480 = 3

First Fragment 1480 + 20, offset 0 and MF bit = 1

Second fragment 1480+20, offset = 1480/8 = 185 , MF =1

Third fragment 1454+20, offset =2960/8 = 370, MF=0

Q6. A link has a MTU of 700 bytes and needs to send datagram of 2400 bytes with 20 bytes as header. Show the fragments, their offset values and more fragment bit.

Ans: Number of bytes that need to be sent are 2400 – 20 = 2380

Data that can maximum be sent in 1 go = 700-20 = 680

No of fragments required = 2380/680 = 4

First Fragment 680+20, offset 0 MF=1

Second Fragment 680+20, offset 680/8 = 85, MF =1

Third Fragment 680+20, offset = 1360/8=170, MF =1

Fourth Fragment 340 + 20, offset=2040/8 = 255, MF =0

Q7. How many datagrams are required to send an MP3 consisting of 4 million bytes if the IP header takes 20 bytes, TCP header takes 20 bytes and MTU is 1500 bytes?

Ans: In each datagram we can carry 1500-40 = 1460 bytes

Number of fragments required = $4 \times 10^6 / 1460$

$$= 2740$$

All datagrams will be of size 1500,

the last one will be of

2739 x 1460 = 3998940

4000000 – 3998940 = 1060

$$= 1060+40$$

$$= 1100 \text{ bytes.}$$

Q8. A bit stream 1101011011 is transmitted using the standard CRC method. The key is 10011. What is the actual bit string transmitted?

Ans:

- If key is 10011.

- Then (k-1) zeros to be appended to the bit string

- Thus a string of 4 zeroes is added at the end of the bit stream which needs to be transmitted.
- Which becomes 11010110110000.

Now, the binary division is performed as-

```
10011 | 1 1 0 1 0 1 1 0 1 10 0 0 0
       1 0 0 1 1
       ________________________

       0 1 0 0 1 1
         1 0 0 1 1
       ________________________

         0 0 0 0 0 1
           0 0 0 0 0
       ________________________

           0 0 0 1 0
             0 0 0 0
       ________________________

             0 0 1 0 1
               0 0 0 0
       ________________________

               0 1 0 1 1
                 0 0 0 0 0
       ________________________

                 1 0 1 1 0
                 1 0 0 1 1
       ________________________

                   0 0 1 0 1 0
                     0 0 0 0 0
       ________________________

                       1 0 1 0 0
                       1 0 0 1 1
       ________________________

                         0 0 1 1 1 0
                           0 0 0 0 0
       ________________________

                           1 1 1 0 ( Remainder)
```

Here CRC = 1110

- The last 4 zeroes of 11010110110000 are replaced with the CRC.
- So this becomes = 11010110111110.
- Which is finally transmitted.

Q9. Obtain the CRC for a string of bits 10110011wih a divisor of 10011

Ans: String 10110011

Divisor 10011

Divisor has k bits = 5

Append the given string with k-1 zeros

So 4 zeros are added to 10110011

Which becomes 101100110000

On Dividing

```
10011 | 1 0 1 1 0 0 1 1 0 0 0 0
          1 0 0 1 1
        ___________________________
            0 0 1 0 1 0
            0 0 0 0 0
        ___________________________
              1 0 1 0 1
              1 0 0 1 1
        ___________________________
                0 0 1 1 0 1
                0 0 0 0 0
        ___________________________
                  1 1 0 1 0
                  1 0 0 1 1
        ___________________________
                    0 1 0 0 1 0
                    1 0 0 1 1
        ___________________________
                      0 0 0 0 1 0
                      0 0 0 1 0 0 (CRC or Remainder )
```

Q10. Compute the checksum for a bit string 100110011110001000100100100000100 using 8 bits

Ans : dividing the string into 8 bit words

10011001 11100010 00100100 10000100

```
    1 0 0 1 1 0 0 1
    1 1 1 0 0 0 1 0
    0 0 1 0 0 1 0 0
    1 0 0 0 0 1 0 0
    _______________
    1 0 0 0 1 0 0 0 1 1
```

There are 2 extra bits so they will be wrapped around

0 0 1 0 0 0 1 1

    1 0

---

0 0 1 0 0 1 0 1Now taking 1s complement1 1 0 1 1 0 1 0

So the checksum is 11011010

At the receiver side the checksum is transmitted to the receiverAll the segments are added with the checksum value0 0 1 0 0 1 0 1 (Addition of 4 segments from above)

1 1 0 1 1 0 1 0 (Adding checksum to them)

---

1 1 1 1 1 1 1 1Taking 1s complement again

0 0 0 0 0 0 0 0

All zeros , so no error

Q11. Suppose 4 frames are sent as follows which ae 8 bits long

11001100, 10101010, 11110000 and 11000011.

At the receiver side they are received as follows

11001100, 10101010, 11110000 and 11001100.

Show with the checksum method how the error is detected.

Ans: Adding 4 segments on sender side

1 1 0 0 1 1 0 0

1 0 1 0 1 0 1 01 1 1 1 0 0 0 01 1 0 0 0 0 1 1.

---

0 1 0 1 0 0 1

    1 1 (two extra bits are wrapped around)

---

0 0 1 0 1 1 0 0 (final sum)

Taking 1s complement1 1 0 1 0 0 1 1 (Checksum)

Adding on receiver side, the 4 segments

1 1 0 0 1 1 0 0

1 0 1 0 1 0 1 0

1 1 1 1 0 0 0 0

1 1 0 0 1 1 0 0 (see this segment has changed as to what was on sender side)

---

0 1 0 1 0 0 1 0

    1 1 0 (wrapped around values)

---

0 1 0 1 1 0 0 0 (sum)

Adding sum and checksum

0 1 0 1 1 0 0 0

1 1 0 1 0 0 1 1 (Checksum)

———————————————————————————————————————

1 0 0 1 0 1 0 1 1

Taking 1s complement

0 1 1 0 1 0 1 0 0 (not all zeros , therefore error introduced)

Q12. A host has an IP address as 189.34.65.175/26

Find the subnet mask

Ans: /26 means 26 1s from the most significant byte

11111111.11111111.11111111.11000000

Translated into decimal

255.255.255.192

Q13. Two networks have a subnet mask of

a) 255.255.0.0

b) 255.255.255.0

Tell the maximum number of hosts that can be accommodated on both.

Ans: a)   255.255.0.0It has 16 bits for network id and 16 bits for host ids

11111111.11111111.00000000.00000000

So maximum hosts can be 2^{16} -2b)   255.255.255.0

It has 24 bits for network id and 8 bits for host id

11111111.11111111.11111111.00000000So maximum number of hosts
can be 2^8 -2 = 256 – 2= 254

**Q14. Write the IP address 187.24.25.98 mask 255.255.255.224 in CIDR
notation**

Ans: Converting 255.255.255.224 in binary is

11111111.11111111.11111111.11100000

255 means all 1s in the octet (11111111)

224 = 128 + 64 + 32 means 3 1s in octet (11100000)

Counting the number of 1s from most significant bit =

8+8+8+3 = 27

Therefore IP address in CIDR notation is

187.24.25.98/27

Q15. Suppose you have an IP address 210.8.11.0 of class C type of network and you have 30 subnets.

a) Give the subnet mask for maximum number of hosts

b) How many hosts can each subnet have

c) What is the IP address of host 3 on subnet 2

Ans: Class C network means subnet mask is 255.255.255.0

We want 30 subnets so 30 will be accommodated in 2^5 bits (32 bits)

Taking 5 most significant bits from the last octet for subnets

So our subnet mask will become

11111111.11111111.11111111.11111000

255.255.255.248

Each subnet will have maximum $2^3 - 2$ hosts = 8-2 = 6 hosts

Subnet 2 means if 5 bits are reserved for subnet then 2 will be represented as

00010

And host 3 means if 3 bits are reserved for hosts then 3 will be represented as

011

Combining both of them for the last octet means

00010011 = 19

So IP address becomes 210.8.11.19

Q16. Suppose we have a class C IP address, we want to accommodate 2 subnets, each being able to accommodate 52 hosts. Write the possible subnet masks.

Ans: Class C type network means we have subnet mask of 255.255.255.0

If we need 2 subnets then we need 1 bit to represent

and to accommodate 52 hosts we will need 26 = (64) values

so our subnet mask will be

11111111.11111111.11111111.10000000

And

11111111.11111111.11111111.11000000

Which represented in decimal are

255.255.255.128 and 255.255.255.192

Q17. Suppose we have a class A network 23.0.0.0. We want to create 8 subnets. Give their addresses in CIDR format.

Ans: 23.0.0.0

To create 8 subnets , we will have to take 3 bits from the host part and give it to network part. And the rest of the 5 bits in the octet will remain 0s. So the network addresses will be as follows:

Subnet 0: 000 00000 -0

Subnet 1 :001 00000 -32

Subnet 2: 010 00000 -64

Subnet 3: 011 00000 -96 (64+32)

Subnet 4: 100 00000 - 128

Subnet 5: 101 00000 - 160 (128+32)

Subnet 6: 110 00000 - 192(128+64)

Subnet 7: 111 00000 - 224(128+64+32)

Therefore the 8 subnet addresses can be written as follows in CIDR format:

23.0.0.0/11

23.32.0.0/11

23.64.0.0/11

23.96.0.0/11

23.128.0.0/11

23.160.0.0/11

23.192.0.0./11

23.224.0.0/11

Q18. Suppose we have an IP address of class C network as 213.223.85.165. If no subnetting is done , what network is it on? How many networks of this class are possible? If we break in 4 subnets , what will be their addresses? How many possible hosts can be in each subnet?

Ans: If no subnetting is done, then it will be on network 213.223.85.0/24

Possible networks of this class are 2^{21} -2

since 1st 3 bits are reserved for class C as 110 and out of 24 bits we can use 21 bits.

To create 4 subnets, we will require only 2 bits from the host part and 6 bits will remain for hosts, so our last octet will be like this:

00 000000 (0)

01 000000 (64)

10 000000 (128)

11 000000 (192)

So their addresses are

213.223.85.0/26

213.223.85.64/26

213.223.85.128/26

213.223.85.192/26

Number of possible hosts in each network are 2^6 = 64 -2 = 62

Q19. Suppose I have an IP address of 192.168.0.0 and I need only 20 hosts. Give the subnet mask that can be used and the possible values for hosts.

Ans: For 20 hosts I can have a subnet mask as 255.255.255.224

11111111.11111111.11111111.11100000

So possible values of hosts can be from

192.168.0.225 to 192.168.0.254,

where 192.168.0.224 and 192.168.0.255 are reserved for network id and broadcast address respectively.

Q20. Consider two hosts connected together by link with a rate of 2Mbps separated by 300m, the speed of propagation is 2 x 10⁸ m/s. If host A sends a packet of size 400bits. Then Calculate the

a) Propagation delay

b) Transmission delay

c) End to end delay (ignoring processing delay)

Propagation delay = distance / speed

$$= 300 \text{ m} / 2 \times 10^8 \text{ m/s}$$

$$= 150 \times 10^{-8} \text{ s}$$

$$= 0.0015 \times 10^{-3} \text{ s}$$

$$= 0.0015 \text{ milliseconds}$$

Transmission delay = Length / Rate

$$= 400 \text{ bits} / 2 \times 10^6 \text{ bits/sec}$$

$$= 200 \times 10^{-6\backslash}$$

$$= 0.2 \times 10^{-3}$$

$$= 0.2 \text{ milliseconds}$$

End to End delay = propagation delay + transmission delay

$$= 0.0015 + 0.2 \text{ milliseconds}$$

$$= 0.2015 \text{ milliseconds}$$

Q21. A datagram of 4000 bytes arrive (20 bytes for IP header and 3980 bytes of IP payload) arrives at a router and must be forwarded to a link of MTU 1500 bytes. Original datagram is stamped with an identification number of 777. How many fragments will be done with the router? What will be size of the fragment, identification, offset and value of flag field in each fragment.

Datagram = 4000 bytes

$$= 3980 + 20$$

MTU = 1500 bytes

ID = 777

Data to be sent in 1 go = 1480 (1500 – 20)

Fragments required = 3980 / 1480

$$= 2.6$$

$$= 3$$

Size of each fragment	identification	offset	value of flag
1480 + 20	777	0	MF = 1
1480 + 20	777	1480/ 8 = 185	MF = 1
1020 = 20	777	2960/8 = 370	MF = 0

Q22. Find out the network address, broadcasting address, first usable host and last usable host address for the following Ips,

a) 154.92.108.90/20

b) 176.126.226.203/25

a) 154.92.108.90/20

The subnet mask for the above is

11111111.11111111.11110000.00000000

The first two octets are reserved for net id since they are all 1s.

The last octet is for host ids since it is all 0s

Taking the 3rd octet, where 4 most significant bits are for network ids and last 4 bits for host ids.

Converting 3rd octet number 108 to binary 01101100

So the network id part is 01100000 which is number 96 in decimal.

Therefore the network id becomes 154.92.96.0

The first usable address will be 154.92.96.1

(11111111.11111111.01100000.00000001)

The last usable address will be 154.92.111.254

(11111111.11111111.01101111.11111110)

The broadcast address would be 154.92.111.255

b) 176.126.226.203/25

The subnet mask for the above is

11111111.11111111.11111111.10000000

The first three octets are reserved for net id since they are all 1s.

Taking the fourth octet, in which only first most significant bit is reserved fornetwork id and last 7 bits for host ids.

Converting 203 to binary is equal to 11001011,

So the network part is 10000000 = 128

The network id therefore becomes 176.126.226.128

The first usable host is 176.126.226.129

The last usable host is 176.126.226.254

The broadcast address is 176.126.226.255

Q23. What is the Total delay(Latency) for a frame size of 10 million bits that is being sent up on link with 15 routers each having queuing time of 2 micro sec and a processing time of 1 micro sec? The length of the link is 3000km. The speed of light inside the link is 2 x 10^8 m/sec. The link has bandwidth of 6Mbps.

Ans: Latency =propagation time +transmission time +queuing time + processing delay

Processing delay =15x1 µs

$$= 15 \text{ µs}$$

$$= 0.000015\text{s}$$

Queuing time = 15x2 μs

$$= 30 \text{ μs}$$

$$= 0.000030s$$

Transmission time = 10000000/6Mbps

$$=1.66s$$

Propagation time = $3000 \times 10^3 / 2 \times 10^8$

$$= 0.015s$$

Latency = 0.000015+0.000030+1.66+0.015

$$=1.6750s$$

Q24. Consider an IP packet with a length of 4500 bytes that include a 20 byte IPv4 header and a 40 byte TCP header. The packet is forwarded to an IPv4 router that supports a Maximum Transmission Unit (MTU) of 600 bytes. Assume that the length of the IP header in all the outgoing fragments of this packet is 20 bytes. Assume that the fragmentation offset value stored in the first fragment is 0. What is the value of fragmentation offset in the 3rd fragment?

Ans: Length of packet is 4500 bytes

Subtracting the IP header of 20 bytes, we have 4500 – 20 = 4480 bytes to transfer.

MTU is of size of 600 bytes.

Subtracting header length, 600 – 20 = 580 bytes.

Fragments needed = 4480 / 580 = 7.72 (in other words 8)

580 is not a multiple of 8, so actual bytes sent will be 576, which is a multiple of 8 closets to 580.

Size of each fragment and offset :

Fragment no	Bytes sent	Offset
1	576	0
2	1152	576/8 = 72
3	1728	1152/8 = 144

And so on ....

So the answer to above question is 144.

Q25. A 3000 km long trunk operates at 1.536 Mbps and is used to transmit 64 bytes frames and uses sliding window protocol. The time taken to propagate 1 km is 6 micro seconds. Calculate the transmission delay and propagation delay.

Transmission Delay = packet size / bandwidth

$\qquad$ = 64 bytes/ 1.536 Mbps

$\qquad$ = 64 * 8 /1.536 * 10^6 seconds

$\qquad$ = 333.33 micro seconds

Propagation Delay = distance / speed

$\qquad$ = the time taken to propagate 1 km is 6 micro seconds

$\qquad$ = the time taken to propagate 3000 km is

$\qquad$ = 3000 * 6 micro seconds= 18000 micro seconds.

NOTES